Cultural Dive
Inclusion in Ea
Education

Cult
how
Ackı
iden
ate ı

A
relat
prov
resp
from

* pı
* sc
* bι
* thı
* en

Inclu
readiı
titionı
childr

Penny
Studiε

Diversity and Inclusion in the Early Years

Cultural Diversity and Inclusion in Early Years Education

Penny Borkett

Routledge
Taylor & Francis Group

LONDON AND NEW YORK

First published 2018
by Routledge
2 Park Square, Milton Park, Abingdon, Oxon OX14 4RN

and by Routledge
711 Third Avenue, New York, NY 10017

Routledge is an imprint of the Taylor & Francis Group, an informa business

© 2018 Penny Borkett

British Library Cataloguing in Publication Data
A catalogue record for this book is available from the British Library

Library of Congress Cataloging in Publication Data
Names: Borkett, Penny, author.
Title: Cultural diversity and inclusion in early years education / Penny Borkett.
Description: Abingdon, Oxon; New York, NY: Routledge, 2018. | Includes
    bibliographical references.
Identifiers: LCCN 2017047598| ISBN 9781138218543 (hardback) | ISBN
    9781138218550 (pbk.) | ISBN 9781315437453 (ebk)
Subjects: LCSH: Early childhood education—Social aspects. |
    Multiculturalism—Study and teaching (Early childhood) | Inclusive
    education.
Classification: LCC LB1139.23 .B67 2018 | DDC 372.21—dc23
LC record available at https://lccn.loc.gov/2017047598

ISBN: 978-1-138-21854-3 (hbk)
ISBN: 978-1-138-21855-0 (pbk)
ISBN: 978-1-315-43745-3 (ebk)

Typeset in Optima
by Swales & Willis Ltd, Exeter, Devon, UK

I dedicate this book to all of the many children and families that I have worked with, recognising all that they have taught me about diversity and difference. Thank you to Peter Eggington who created the diagrams. I especially thank Mary and Hannah for their support of me throughout their lives, my gorgeous grandchildren Evie, Bethany and Oliver for all that they continually teach me about being young, and to Phill, who has always encouraged me to strive on without giving up. Finally thanks to God for his guidance throughout my life.

Contents

Acknowledgements

Through this book case studies have been included, many of which are situations and challenges that I have met during my 20-year career of working with families. Many of them involve children who will now be entering adult life and I hope that the way myself and others worked with them in their early years has had a positive impact on their lives. I have to thank my colleagues who worked with me in a range of Sure Start children's centres across the Midlands and West Yorkshire and my current colleagues working on the foundation degree in early years and the BA (Hons) team working on early childhood and childhood studies degrees at Sheffield Hallam University. Your patience and support has been immense. I should also thank the many students that I meet along the way in my current role, who often challenge my views and cause me to reflect on issues around inclusion.

Finally, thanks to Annamarie Kino and Clare Ashworth from Routledge who have supported me through this entire process.

Glossary

Agency   the opportunity to be able to make a choice between more than one option.

Attachment   a loving and affectionate bond between a baby and their carer.

Bicultural   the combining of two or more cultures.

Cohabitation   living with someone outside of marriage.

Commonwealth   an association of 53 nations, which used to belong to the British empire.

Democracy/democratic   a term that means 'ruled by the people' and is about having the ability to vote and have a voice in decisions that affect us.

Developing world   the nations of the world that are not so economically well developed or technologically advanced.

Early years setting   any setting that accepts children to be cared for and educated between the ages of 0–5. This could be a parent and toddler group, child minder, preschool, maintained nursery or private day nursery.

Ethnography   the recording and analysis of the way a culture or society lives and works, usually based on participant observation and resulting in a written account of a people or place.

Globalisation   the way the world is becoming increasingly interconnected as a result of massively increased trade and cultural exchange.

Holistic development   to simultaneously address the physical, emotional, relational, intellectual and spiritual aspects of a child's life altogether rather than separately.

Home language   the main language used in a person's home, which may be different from the dominant language of a country.

Open-ended resources   materials that can be used in numerous ways indoors and outdoors by babies, toddlers and young children.

Practitioner   a term used to discuss any person who is working in an early years setting. It could be a teacher, qualified nursery nurse or student working on placement towards a qualification in early years.

Refugee   a person who has had to flee their country of origin because of war, political unrest, persecution or natural disaster.

Role model   someone that a child may look up to as a good example of how they might lead their lives.

School council   a group of students who are elected to represent the views of all pupils and to improve their school.

Sure Start   a government programme that provides a range of multi-agency support services for parents and children.

Trafficking   the recruitment, transportation, transfer, harbouring or receipt of people, by means of threat or use of force or other forms of coercion, abduction or fraud.

Introduction

This book relates to children developing in both multicultural and predominantly white communities. All children are unique and need to grow up to understand and embrace this and to acknowledge that all families and children live differently with no one group of people being or seeing themselves as superior to others.

Part I relates to the understanding of some of the background of multiculturalism and why it was important for the government in the 1960s to set up policies that focused on ensuring that children were accepted and welcomed into educational settings. Part I also focuses on what inclusion is and how it affects practitioners and the need for all colleagues to work collectively to ensure true inclusion. It goes on to explore some of the history of policy documents since the 1960s, when the first wave of immigrants began to arrive in the UK.

During this time I was beginning my life at school. I lived in London where a lot of immigrants were placed and for this reason the local authority had built a new estate around the corner from my junior school. I therefore grew up playing and learning with children from lots of cultures. As I grew older I spent time with them either in their homes or mine. I became fascinated with the differences between the way they lived and the way I lived. I think this is the reason for my fascination of people wherever they come from and whatever needs they may have.

Part I of the book also discusses some of the sociocultural theories. It focuses on four theorists examining some of, what might be for you, new concepts and principles that could be used in practice. The last chapter in this part focuses on the importance of children knowing their identity and the role that culture takes in this.

Part II of the book focuses on the more practical aspects of working with families and their children. It first discusses the need to work alongside parents and families in a non-judgemental and sensitive way, particularly if they are new to the UK and may not be used to early education or indeed the way that children are educated through play. It discusses differences in the way that all families live their lives and makes suggestions as to how practitioners may get alongside families and share views in a non-discriminatory way. The final chapter discusses working alongside children. Again it focuses on strategies that can be used in practice to ensure that all children are included and that enable them to have a voice in decisions that affect them.

It is important to acknowledge that during the process of writing this book the UK has entered a period of instability. The referendum in the UK in 2016, which determined whether or not Britain remained in the European Union (EU), cited the immigration to the UK from people across the world and Europe as one of the main reasons why Britain should leave the EU. Across the world evidence of terrorism is increasing and this too makes society uncomfortable about high levels of immigration. Yet the media recognises that often immigrants will do the work in the UK that British people refuse to. Asian people are currently seeing a rise in hate crimes so perhaps this is a time in our country's history when a book that seeks to celebrate cultural diversity while also acknowledging at times its challenges, is needed. The politician Jo Cox made the claim before her murder in 2016 that 'we have far more in common than the issues that divide us' and I hope that this book recognises this and encourages early years practitioners to celebrate the diversity in us all. It is so important that from an early age children seek to recognise diversity and difference in a positive way as they will then go on to be adults who recognise difference as vibrant and exciting.

Within each chapter there are both case studies and areas for reflection. These can be used in two ways. If you are a lecturer using this book for teaching, either the case studies or reflection points could be used with students to encourage discussion and reflection on information given in the book. If you are reading this as a student, it might be good for you to note down your reaction to some of the information, case studies and reflections in the book.

Also in the chapters are suggestions of resources and strategies that can be used in practice in both early years settings or individually with children. These strategies, in the main, will go towards ensuring good practice in your setting. Although there has not been sufficient room in this book to discuss good practice in any depth, any strategy that supports inclusion, transition, communication and aids practitioners in developing their ways of working will ensure that your setting is on its way to being an inclusive one, which is a very good thing.

Part I

Chapter 1 seeks to attempt to answer the question what is inclusion? Inclusion, in my experience, is one of those concepts that is much discussed in early years settings but is quite hard to orchestrate. The chapter considers the importance of the 'unique' child, one of the four main principles of the Early Years Foundation Stage (EYFS), which was established by the Department for Children, Schools and Families (DCSF) in 2008 and how this views all children as competent and capable whatever their ethnicity, ability, gender, language abilities or culture.

The chapter then continues to consider how inclusion has changed over the years from previously being in the main related to Special Educational Needs (SEN) and how more recently it relates to all areas of inclusion and, particularly in the context of this book, cultural diversity. The chapter will challenge practitioners to see diversity and difference as exciting and something that should be considered as a resource rather than dividing children.

Various strategies and ways of working such as the Index for Inclusion are introduced and discussed in the light of the need for all members of a staff team to come together strategically to discuss how the setting can become more inclusive. This should include staff who may not be part of the 'on-hand' teaching team and who at times are seen as being more on the periphery of the staff, such as midday supervisors and caretakers. Other strategies that are introduced are personal passports. These focus on how information can be shared by family and practitioners during times of transition. Kolb's reflective cycle is discussed as it works well alongside the EYFS planning cycle to reflect on challenging situations in settings. Makaton, a sign language that supports both children with SEN and those who may be bilingual, is introduced and discussed. The role of the equalities named co-ordinator (ENCO) whose purpose is to ensure that the cultural elements of families are welcomed and celebrated in settings will also be identified and discussed. Finally the differing views of parents in relation to education is also discussed in a way that emphasises the need to try and understand why it is that some parents prefer their children to learn to read and write when young instead of playing.

Any book that focuses on the needs of families and children should also consider the role of policy and how this impacts on practice in settings. Chapter 2 spends time inviting the reader to discover the importance of policies and to consider some of the history of well-known policies, and why they needed to be written and implemented. The chapter goes on to discuss some of the historical aspects of immigration in the UK and how policy was established in the 1960s when the first wave of immigrants came over to the UK. These policies were orchestrated to assist teachers and practitioners in working with families from diverse cultures. The Plowden Report is extolled as this introduced the importance of early years education to young children in the UK, and although written in the 1960s is still very relevant today, particularly in relation to those coming from other cultures as well as those living in areas of deprivation. The Swann Report is also considered, as although initiated in 1985, this policy sets out recommendations that are still important some 30 years later. The Report supports the need for practitioners to be trained about other cultures in order to gain a deeper awareness of the lives and traditions of families as well as extolling the opportunities for diversity to be a teaching tool rather than something that divides groups.

The United Nations Convention on the Rights of the Child is examined, as this was an important human rights treaty, which sought to ensure that children across the world have the same rights and entitlements. However, documents such as these also divide opinion, as it can be argued that it is not possible for all children across the world to have the same rights and entitlements when they live in different environments. These views will be discussed and the reader will be challenged to consider these dilemmas.

Finally this chapter seeks to unpick the evolving journey of the Early Years Foundation Stage, which was orchestrated in 2008. It discusses the many changes that this policy has been through between 2008 and 2017 and the Prevent Duty, which became part of it in 2015.

Chapter 3 considers the role of theory and cultural diversity and particularly examines the views of four people. It is important that rather than introducing theories in specific chapters all four are introduced at the beginning of the book. The first to be discovered is Jerome Bruner who as the oldest of the theorists is recognised as a social constructivist. Bruner held the view that children's development is not only about what the child learns naturally and within the constraints of their age, but is also affected by society and the customs and traditions of the family in which the child develops and grows. Bruner views culture as an essential aspect of their lives. He identifies the role of the practitioner as essential in giving focus to the culture of the child. Bruner believed that children develop through three particular modes and views adults as essential to the way that a child develops, communicates and learns. Bruner is also well known for his views on the use of language as a tool for learning and how practitioners can encourage this in their interactions with children. The chapter also identifies Bruner's view on the 'spiral curriculum', which is used to revisit topics, subjects or themes throughout the child's life course.

The chapter then continues to introduce Bronfenbrenner's ecological systems theory. This theory views the child and family as central to society and sees development as a continual relationship between the, as he views it, four main layers of society. The theory is represented in many ways through concentric circles where each layer relates to the next. It therefore views life as forever evolving and being dependent on society, government policy and international changes.

The third theory to be recognised is that of an American called Barbara Rogoff. Rogoff as with Bruner postulates the need for practitioners to consider the culture, traditions and faith journeys of the family in which a child grows and views these as vital to a child's life. Rogoff is known as being a sociocultural theorist who views the role of practitioners as being essential to a child's development. She also recognises other people in children's lives as offering 'guided participation' to children while in the home, suggesting that these might be family members, relatives such as grandparents and siblings as well as community elders and religious leaders who may have an impact on the family.

Rogoff introduces the notion of cultural tools and suggests that early years practitioners should give careful thought to ensuring that cultural tools do not only represent the dominant culture of the setting but also other cultures that might be represented.

The final theorist that the chapter introduces is Liz Brooker, who like Rogoff has carried out research across the world to examine the impact of culture to a child. She, along with Bruner and Rogoff, views the cultural upbringing of a child to be a central tenet to their lives and has first-hand knowledge of how this impacts on families through her research. Brooker's research is often ethnographic, meaning that she carries out her research in multicultural areas and strives to understand differences in views of the role of education in families' lives. She has particularly carried out research about families' views of play and its role in teaching young children. It is important to address this as it has the potential to divide opinion in settings. The chapter then focuses on Brooker's triangle of care, which examines opportunities that the child, family and practitioner have to work in true partnership for the good of all concerned.

Chapter 4 focuses more on the child, while first seeking to answer the question 'what is a child?' It focuses on the view that opinions relating to the child and childhood will depend on the culture and everyday experiences that a child grows up in. The chapter considers issues around a child's identity and attempts to decipher what certain words mean. Terms such as 'identity', 'culture', 'religion' and 'spirituality' are unpicked in order to better understand some of these concepts used in relation to young children.

The chapter goes on to consider how children begin to form ideas about their own identity and who and what they are and discusses issues that can permeate a child's life and negatively impact on the child's view of themselves. It explains how negative issues such as racism can affect a child and also views how children are represented by the media and how this might impact on a child's view of their identity. The chapter identifies the impact of parents and how they can unknowingly negatively affect the child. The chapter then introduces the term 'tokenism' to the reader. Tokenism is when a person or setting portrays a culture in a limited way, not really understanding the intricacies of culture. This too can have a negative impact on the understanding of children and the way they view children from other cultures.

Part II

Chapter 5 focuses on the role of the family, first considering what a family is and exploring how the family has changed over the past 50 years. While discussing the role of the family, consideration is given to the notion that families across the world rear their children very differently. It is vital that early years practitioners recognise this and rather than judging them, seek to understand why this might be. The chapter then seeks to unpick certain terms used, particularly in the media, to describe people coming to the UK from across the world. A term known as 'cultural intelligence' (CQ) is introduced and is discussed in order to inform practitioners of how it can be used to view and understand the way that people live and work through a cultural lens. It goes on to discuss policy requirements around working with families and how this particularly has an impact on the need to safeguard children and families. Finally, the chapter discusses the important role of the key/bilingual worker in supporting families and working alongside them in order to understand their way of life and to break down any barriers relating to cultural awareness.

Chapter 6 examines ways of working with young children in order that they may grow up to positively accept each other as unique. The chapter begins with the enabling environment and the acknowledgement of the importance of the environment and the way that it gives children cues about what each area is for, and how they can best use the resources and environment that has been created. It goes on to discuss the importance of using culture as a resource and not something that differentiates groups of children. A large section of the chapter discusses and explains communication and the importance of ensuring a range of communication within the environment of both the dominant and other cultures. It introduces the terms 'agency' and 'participation' and how both of these concepts can encourage children to become democratic beings. The term 'augmentative communication' is introduced, which covers forms of non-spoken communication, and the chapter discusses that children do not just communicate orally but through signs, symbols, drawing, IT and also through their body language. Finally, the chapter discusses the many benefits and challenges of bilingualism and how practitioners can support and encourage bilingual children.

The final chapter brings the book to its conclusion and also makes suggestions of organisation, resources and activities that the reader can examine in order to make their practice more inclusive. I hope that the book will be a useful resource to all of those who seek to ensure that children are supported to view diversity and difference in a positive way.

Understanding the issues

What is inclusion?

Introduction

This chapter will discuss the evolving, organic nature of inclusion as well as analysing differences between the terms 'integration' and 'inclusion', considering how these concepts have changed over the years. It will examine the principle of 'the unique child' as set out through the Early Years Foundation Stage document (DCSF 2008) and how this encompasses all areas of inclusion and views all children as unique, rather than viewing inclusion as being about certain groups of children. The United Nations Convention on the Rights of the Child (UNCRC) Article 28 sets out that all children 'have the right to an education' (Unicef 1989), and Article 29 goes on to state that education should develop respect for human rights in the child. On this basis, it is important that from the very start of a child's life they should be equipped to recognise difference in a positive way. The discussion will then move on to the notion that, in order to establish a wholly inclusive setting, the entire staff team need to be involved, while deliberating on the view that this may include people who would not ordinarily be involved in such discussions. The promotion of the value of documents such as the Index for Inclusion (CSIE 2004) is considered and the role of reflective practice, which can assist settings to question and make changes to current practice and promote an inclusive ethos, is also discussed.

Alongside this, the chapter discusses the need for practitioners to consider their own views of inclusion in an open and non-threatening way. As Baldock suggests (2010), rather than being 'silenced' practitioners should be encouraged to talk about deep-seated views and prejudices that they may have, which might influence their practice. The final section discusses strategies that can be used in settings to reflect the diversity of the world whether or not the setting is in a multicultural area.

What is meant by the term 'inclusion'?

'Inclusion' is a much contested, multifaceted term, which has evolved over the years. In the past, the term 'integration' was more likely to be used when considering the education of those who were seen as 'different' from the norm. Savage (2015, p. 4) discusses the view that integration was often related to people who appeared to be 'outsiders' or who were excluded from society in some way. Rix (2011), when identifying integration suggests that practitioners often acknowledge the 'dominant culture' of their setting while failing to acknowledge other cultures that should also be represented. For instance, a setting that is in a predominantly white area may not acknowledge the need to represent other cultures, as no families from these are present in the setting. According to Corbett (2001), integration was more concerned with adaptations to existing practice and the notion that a child had to 'fit in' with the practice of the setting. However, in my view all children are part of a multicultural society and need to acknowledge difference and diversity in order to learn that everyone is unique whether they live in a multicultural community or not. Rix also suggests that practitioners may consider groups of people who seem to be different according to their own stereotypes, which often permeate society. This is sometimes known as the 'deficit' model, which views certain groups of people as being less important than others. Children can be disadvantaged for many reasons but for the purpose of this book, I will be discussing particularly the needs of children from different ethnic backgrounds and children who may linguistically appear different.

The concept of the 'unique child' as one of the four main principles of the Early Years Foundation Stage (EYFS) introduced by the Department for Children, Schools and Families (DCSF) in 2008, asserted the view that practitioners should value the diversity of all individuals. It also sought to ensure that communities are valued and respected, and that nobody is discriminated against. This view is replicated through the UN Convention on the Rights of the Child (Unicef 1989), Article 2, which states that each child should be free of discrimination with particular regard to their 'race, colour, language, faith, national, ethnic or social origin'.

It is important to consider that children can be discriminated against in two ways. First, they may be discriminated against indirectly. An example of this would be if a setting does not have a written policy around equality and discrimination. This might suggest that they have never considered that children are unique and so require differentiated planning that might require different strategies and resources in order to thrive and learn. They can also be discriminated against directly. This may be apparent if a setting becomes aware that certain groups of children will be coming into the setting from a different culture and they do not make changes to their practice or resources as a result of this. If these kinds of discrimination are experienced in early years settings, how much more are they experienced within society? Children absorb ideas around discrimination from their parents and immediate family, their peers, situations in their community and society and from the media and TV. All of these can have an impact on how children see and treat each other. In order for children to learn and thrive they need to be in a state of emotional well-being and feel secure wherever they are. A child who may experience discrimination may not feel like this.

Returning to the term 'inclusion', Nutbrown and Clough (2009) stress that in the past the term was used more in relation to children with special educational needs (SEN), but the term is now considered to be about all areas of childhood. It incorporates ability, ethnic and linguistic background, gender and faith. Corbett (2001) views inclusion as an emancipatory concept that relates to the empowerment of people encouraging and celebrating difference and diversity in all.

Savage (2015) takes Corbett's views one stage further by suggesting that inclusion should be part of 'a healthy instinct in a strong confident society' (p. 5). Levitas (1998) picks up this view postulating that inclusion is an important element of social inclusion. I would support this view as children who grow up to value difference as something to be discussed and celebrated are more likely to grow into adults who recognise diversity as a natural part of society; thus being more likely to stand up for injustice when they view situations that relate to prejudice. Aboud *et al.* (2012) comment that treating others differently because of their ethnic background can lead to 'name calling and social exclusion' (p. 308). However, while I agree that issues around children's prejudices must always be challenged, for me part of being an inclusive practitioner is about embracing diversity, while encouraging children to discuss differences in an open and supportive way, seeing diversity as an opportunity to encourage children to learn about difference positively. Araujo and Strasser (2003) agree that while encouraging practitioners to celebrate cultural diversity with children they should also 'help them to see their common bonds' (p. 180) and to use these as a resource for teaching.

Nutbrown and Clough (2009) also view inclusion as a human right for all, discussing its importance to a child's identity while arguing that if a child's culture is not valued this may lead to the child feeling isolated, which may then go on to affect their self-esteem. Moss (2007) views inclusion as a democratic right for all children and challenges practitioners to rethink their policies and practices to ensure that the rights of all children are met. Beneke and Cheatham (2015) concur, and discuss how practitioners should value and celebrate children's linguistic and cultural identities, as these are an important element of their emerging identities. It is vital that children feel they belong in a setting, and that their identity is valued. Children need practitioners who will encourage positive interactions with one another, encouraging children to talk about and discuss their feelings. They need practitioners who encourage and challenge children to resolve their differences openly and in a sensitive way. However, doing this is not always easy, sometimes practitioners have very different understandings of the term 'inclusion' or have had personal situations that may hamper their ability to think in an inclusive way. To create truly inclusive practice requires a whole-team approach where views can be discussed and contested in an open forum, led by a practitioner who can sensitively challenge ideals and situations. Only when a whole team can understand and deliver inclusive practice will children truly value the importance of who they are.

Reflection points

- How might you define the term 'inclusion'?

- Do you think that practitioners in your setting agree on what inclusion is?

- How might practice in your setting change from integration to inclusion?

- How might you begin to change practice in your setting in order to make it more inclusive to all?

Case study 1.1

About 15 years ago I started studying on a Master's-level programme around inclusive practice. At the time I was working in a local authority (LA) as a portage worker. Whilst my belief is that inclusion is vital to all children, particularly whilst they are in their formative years, I do accept that there are, and always will be, particular children for whom a special school better meets their needs. I was concerned that this programme of education may change my views.

One of the services that the local authority offered to families of children with special needs was a playgroup, which was open two mornings a week. This had been established by the local Down Syndrome Association and then also opened up to children with other disabilities. Part of my role was to oversee this group and the planning of activities for the individual needs of the children concerned.

I immediately faced a personal dilemma. I was running this group for children who I believed should have been in a mainstream setting. The group followed as much as possible the Early Years Foundation Stage, yet it was not totally inclusive because all of the children had some kind of special need. The LA discussed this group at length and I had the opportunity to share my views. It was decided by the SEN team that although the setting was not inclusive to all children, the needs of the children attending were so different that the differentiated learning was inclusive in some way. The group continued to run but this dilemma was always in the back of my mind.

As children attending the group started to acquire greater skills the portage team started to work with the early years settings, which would accept the children as they approached 3 years of age. We were able to advise the settings of the kind of provision the children would need, what their interests and fascinations were and the kinds of communication aids that they would need. As the children moved into their mainstream settings staff were well informed of the individual needs of each child, and they knew something of the family circumstances and the skills that the children had. Essentially they knew what the children could do, as well as what they struggled to do.

I started to understand that although the playgroup was not inclusive it did prepare children and families for the mainstream setting that the children entered. I slowly started to realise that the playgroup was an essential place not only for the children but also for the parents who could meet with families who were going through similar dilemmas.

Reflection

- How do you ensure that planning for children in your setting is differentiated and individualised?

- Is it always appropriate for children with special needs to attend mainstream settings?

- How might inclusive settings be of benefit to all children attending?

We are all in this together

I remember a time when I changed job roles. I went from working in a multicultural children's centre to leading a small team in a different centre in another area of the UK where the predominant culture was white British. It felt so different and yet after a while, I realised that there were many similarities between the areas despite the fact that they were culturally very different. I was leading a group of people whose views around diversity were mixed. In addition there were quite traditional prejudices ingrained in the community. Rather than immediately being dictatorial in my views I slowly discussed and in some respects challenged the team to reflect on where their strong views had come from and we worked together to produce policies that embedded inclusive practice, which welcomed all to use the setting and the resources therein. However, if that fundamental belief in inclusion is not echoed at a leadership and strategic level it may be hard to remove existing barriers. Gramelt (2013) discusses research that she carried out in German kindergartens with practitioners around cultural inclusion. Here the researcher discovered a pervading view among practitioners that all children are the same and should be treated equally. They found that some of the settings were 'stereotypical' and formed from 'dominant mono-cultural impressions' (p. 52). I suppose to a certain degree this was the practice that I had experienced when changing settings. Having now moved over to teaching students I see similar views replicated. Often, however, when you delve a little deeper, these views are born from a lack of knowledge around cultural diversity and the worry that practitioners 'do not want to get it wrong and offend certain groups'. Allan (2008, p. 32) endorses this claim by suggesting that 'practitioners' references to inclusion are characterised by a sense of frustration, guilt, exhaustion and moral panic'.

What can practitioners do to try and change practice in relation to diversity?

So how do practitioners get over these hurdles and view difference as something positive? Over 10 years ago the Centre for Studies on Inclusive Education (2004) produced the Index for Inclusion. This document encourages settings to look beyond categories of inclusion and to ensure that practice is appropriate for all children and practitioners. It encourages a whole-team approach to address issues of diversity, which could include people who may feel that they are on the periphery of an early years team, such as midday supervisors, caretakers, office staff and students on placement. The Index encourages all to discuss the ethos, practice and resources of the setting to ensure that it is fully inclusive. Throughout the Index, there is both discussion and suggestions of how settings can change practice in order to become more inclusive. This can give the opportunity for inclusivity to be truly embedded into practice. The Index extols the need to restructure outdated policies, and to recognise as Nutbrown and Clough (2009) do, that inclusion is a matter of social justice. Corbett (2001) and Baldock (2010) suggest, however, that at times practitioners who are involved in such projects may just be paying 'lip service' (p. 70) to diversity and that the support is in danger of becoming tokenistic. To a certain extent I would agree with this view, however, I also acknowledge that all settings have to start somewhere and sometimes it takes just one person's interest in inclusion to spark the rest of the team to challenge and change practice. If a setting produces new policies, and through these creates an inclusive culture that ensures that their practice is fair to all, they will be well on the way to becoming a setting that welcomes difference and diversity.

Corbett challenges practitioners to think about the individual needs of every child and to ensure that settings become a 'listening community' (2001, p. 95). At times this can be difficult, as practitioners may have deeply held beliefs that need to be challenged, or the way they behave to particular groups of children might need addressing. It may be that old ways of working need to be re-considered, new resources acquired, activities adjusted or that deeply held beliefs be challenged, but this is all part of what becoming an inclusive setting is about.

Case study 1.2

It is dinner time and the children attending either bring a packed lunch from home or have a school lunch that is provided by an outside organisation. The menus indicate that the meal on offer is baked gammon, potatoes and vegetables. Two of the children having lunch are Muslims and therefore do not eat pork of any type so they are told that they will have Quorn – they seem very excited about this.

When the children's dinner appears it is beef rather than pork, which both children would be able to eat. There was a great deal of discussion among the practitioner and midday supervisor as to whether it was appropriate to let the children eat the beef rather than the Quorn. Thus the two children concerned had to wait longer than the others for their dinner.

If a whole-team approach to inclusion had occurred in the setting then issues around cultural differences and food could have been addressed earlier, meaning that the children would have had their meal with all the others.

- What would your view have been about this situation?

- How might you ensure that issues such as this are discussed in an open forum with staff who do not attend the setting for the entire day?

How can families be supported to celebrate cultural diversity?

So far this chapter has, in the main, discussed the needs of children, however, children usually come within a family context and it is vital in inclusive settings that the needs of parents are listened to and accommodated. If inclusion is truly to be a team approach I would suggest that both parents and children are important members of that team. This view is shared by Devarakonda (2013). This can be a challenge as families come from diverse backgrounds and may have very different views about education. These views can sometimes challenge our widely held 'Westernised' views. Some may not value play as being important to a child's learning and would much prefer it if their child were encouraged, at an early age, to read and write. Others who may come from other areas of Europe may not see education as important for children under the age of 5 as their countries of origin may not accept children into formal education until they are 6 or 7. Others may have had a difficult experience of the education system themselves so do not want to be involved with their child's education as they have a fear of what they see as 'school-related' communities. All of these views should be acknowledged, but this needs doing sensitively and in a way that does not offend families. While carrying out research in London, Corbett (2001) discovered that often the most inclusive settings were in multicultural areas of social deprivation where families often found life hard but where there was support within communities to live together accepting and celebrating difference. One such project that is delivered by Save the Children is the FAST (Families and Schools Together) project. This scheme was started in 2009 and seeks to bring parents, teachers and the wider community together to carry out activities that encourage parents to be involved in their child's education while also building up relationships within the community. At the end of each session, the groups share a meal together that has been cooked by parents and this can encourage greater cultural awareness and discussion. Corbett goes on to discuss the reflective nature of settings alongside an awareness and sensitivity for multicultural education.

Reflection points

- How does your setting attempt to build relationships with parents?
- How might you start to discuss differences in views with parents from other cultures?
- How might you start to change practice in your setting with parents?

The place of reflective practice in inclusion

One of the best and most open ways to discuss and disseminate systems in settings is through reflective practice. I have always found this to be a useful tool to discuss situations that arise and evaluate new practices. However, to be truly responsive to practice means that the team needs to be sensitive to the needs of others and, as I have suggested previously, value all those involved in the setting. There are many theories that relate to reflective practice but the one that I feel is most appropriate is Kolb's reflective cycle (1984). This relates well to the early years planning cycle, which was introduced through Development Matters (Early Education 2012) when it was launched as a document for early years educators to use alongside the EYFS. Kolb's cycle encourages practitioners to reflect both during and after situations that occur in practice that need some adjustment. It uses a questioning approach to challenge, analyse and evaluate. However, Brookfield (1998) offers caution to practitioners: the cycle has the power to conflict with practitioners' own belief and value systems, as well as challenging everyday practice and assumptions that may never have been questioned before.

A personal experience of reflective practice

About 12 years ago I found myself in a situation where I needed to use Kolb's cycle in terms of my own practice and that of the staff I was working with. I will demonstrate through this vignette how reflective practice was needed for this challenge. At the time I was studying and had been looking at the benefits of reflective practice as a tool during my study. I decided to use it and do some research of my own to try and understand an ongoing issue in the setting. I hoped that this would give the team greater understanding and view something from the families' perceptions in relation to play.

I was working with a portage team (National Portage Association 2016) in a multicultural area where I spent much of my time visiting families whose children had a special need of some kind. Portage is a home-visiting educational programme that uses play to teach children new skills. Families are a central tenet of the programme as they are encouraged to engage with activities between the fortnightly visits from the portage worker. I began to discover over time that some parents were not engaging with the programme or the toys that I would provide. Alongside this, when groups were put on in the centre for parents from the area they did not seem to engage with the activities provided. The staff were becoming disheartened and felt that the way the setting was working needed changing. Rather than blaming the parents for not understanding how play can help children to learn, I started to do some research with many of the parents that the centre was working with. Some of the team members also wanted to be involved, so it was very much a team project. I encouraged families and staff members to reflect on how they used to play when they were younger and the impact that this had on how they played with their own children. I soon discovered that there were many credible reasons why it was that parents did not seem to engage in play. For some it was because of the cost of toys, this was a very socially deprived area where many of the families were refugees or seeking asylum from their countries of origin. Others did not share the 'Westernised' view that play is a vehicle to children's learning – they saw it as being something that children did once they had done their learning or helped family with chores at the end of the school day. Other families had not had toys themselves as children; they demonstrated to me how they themselves would make toys from things that were available outside. In the light of what I had discovered, the centre slowly changed practice as a result of these discussions. Toys would continue to be used but we also ensured that there were opportunities for children to use more natural resources in their play. At the same time the outside space in the setting was being developed and it was ensured that there were areas in this where children could dig, play with sand and water and help to grow plants and food that the setting would use in their community café.

One week the families were encouraged to make memory keepers from old shoe boxes – the parents not only enjoyed the experience but spent more time involved with their children. Around the same time, treasure baskets and heuristic play were gaining momentum in settings. These types of play encourage the use of natural resources such as wood, sponge, card, rubber, metal and brushes. They encourage babies and small children to use their senses, to investigate and explore and to learn through this exploration. Rather than practitioners viewing play as a problem they now had a greater understanding of the needs of the families and their views in relation to play. We continued to evaluate both home visits and the groups to ensure that what was being provided fitted the needs of all the families in the area.

This example of reflective practice has stayed with me. It is always important to have honest conversations with parents and practitioners in order to offer effective practice that meets the needs of all.

Case study 1.3

A nursery practitioner was going out to do a home visit with a family. Their son (Theo) was around 9 months old and was coming into the setting later on in the term and the practice of the setting was that all children had at least one home visit to discuss with the family the needs of the child as well as sharing the practice of the setting itself.

The parents were born and grew up in Nigeria and moved to the UK recently when the father came here to study. His wife also wanted to return to study. Theo appeared to be a lively little boy who at the time of the visit was standing up and trying to walk around the furniture. He was very inquisitive and interested in all that was going on during the visit. Both parents were present but it seemed to be the father who was asking all the questions. Theo had a few toys around him and some books that he appeared to be enjoying.

After quite a long discussion about the setting and what would happen to Theo while he was there his mother said to the practitioner that she was concerned about her son because 'all he seems to do is play' she continued to discuss how important it was for both her and her husband that the child received a good education in the UK and that this was one of the reasons that they chose to come here. The practitioner sensitively discussed how in the UK play is used to help children's development. She talked about how children's natural explorations and play leads to children learning, especially in areas of literacy and numeracy, discussing how when children move into school they are better equipped to deal with the more formal/academic nature of education. She also showed the family photographs of the setting so that they could see that there was a mixture of activities that Theo could engage with.

- Have you ever been in this kind of situation with a family?

- How would you start to discuss differences in curriculum in this kind of situation?

- What would you ensure was in place in the setting to try and support parents whose views of education are different?

- How might reflective practice help you and your team to address issues like this?

What is good practice?

It is important for practitioners to do the best they can to ensure that wherever possible they offer good practice to all the children and families living in the community. Yet trying to evaluate good practice is not an easy task. It is something that means different things to different people. Kay (2015) suggests that sometimes it is about a particular aspect of practice, at other times it may be more about the 'feel' of a setting when someone goes in for the first time. They would hopefully see the children happy in what they are doing and practitioners alongside the children engaging with them and trying to deepen their knowledge through well-planned and purposeful play. In recent years Ofsted (2015) have suggested areas of good practice might relate to:

- the quality of teaching being of a very high quality;

- practitioners having a clear understanding of how children learn;

- children being provided with rich, varied and imaginative experiences;

- practitioners completing assessments that are precise, fully focused, monitored and used to move the children on in their learning.

Some of this may be hard to achieve when staff working in settings do not have adequate training to deliver high-quality teaching or may never have been taught the importance of enabling environments and the many varied and imaginative experiences children can learn from.

However, it is important that as well as having access to all of the above, children should also be celebrated for their uniqueness and supported if they are falling behind in any area of their development. As those of us who have worked/are working in the early years know, it is an evolving field. It seems that not a year goes by without something new being added to the role of an early years practitioner. The EYFS is constantly changing and being updated and as we shall read later in the book policies are altered due to trends in society. However, it is the practitioners' responsibility to make decisions and judgements about the quality of provision offered in settings. At times as practitioners you may not agree with a certain policy or the way that something is being done in your setting – this I believe is the hallmark of a reflective practitioner. Someone who can see that something needs changing is confident and prepared to make changes after discussion with the staff team.

Strategies that can help to promote inclusive practice

This final part of the chapter will discuss strategies that can be used in all settings in order that they become inclusive to all families whatever their ethnicity.

Personal passports

One of the tools that was used by the portage team in scenarios like Case Study 1.1 was personal passports (Millar 2004). These were developed to be child-centred pictorial information booklets that tell people about the child and elements of their history. They seek to inform people of positive aspects of the child through a booklet that is developed by the parents and the child themselves but put together by the portage worker. Information should be written in a positive way and should include:

- aspects of the child's disabilities and learning needs;

- equipment the child might need to access certain activities;

- how the child communicates and whether they need any particular tools to help them;

- the child's likes and dislikes;

- information about the child's dietary and personal needs.

The information can be supported by photographs of the child, which will help staff to find out a little more about them. These passports proved invaluable to staff in settings to keep them informed of the needs of the child and their family.

These personal passports are a very effective way of sharing information about a child in a positive way.

Another of the most fundamental needs for families and children is the ability to communicate with others. This can be one of the most difficult areas to judge when meeting the needs of families, particularly those from other cultures who may not know English very well. When there are a number of families speaking several different languages in an area, it can be hard to ensure that communication is effective and open. If finances are available, it may be prudent to employ people from the community as bilingual workers. In the setting that I discussed earlier there were 52 different languages spoken in the area so many of the staff reflected this diverse area and spoke two or three languages. This certainly helped. Often local authorities or those linked to the NHS will have links with translation services that can be accessed, however, this is often at a cost to the setting.

For children, the language used in settings can be a real issue particularly if the child's home language is different from that used in the setting. I strongly advise settings to use a sign language such as Makaton (Makaton.org n.d.) with children. Makaton is a language programme that uses signs, symbols and spoken language to communicate and using this may help children's communication to become more effective. In a setting that I visited recently I observed particular adults using Makaton as well as symbols in each of the rooms. In the younger children's room where children were aged from 18 months to 2 years old it was used well. Staff discussed how useful it is, but also put forward the view that as children were in their early stages of communication, with many of them using only single words, it was easier to make themselves understood through their speech. The signs and symbols did, however, seem to give children visual clues to words and the children used the signs with each other particularly in the reading area.

In the rooms for the older children, although the signs and symbols were still apparent, I felt that, in the main, Makaton was used more with children who had special needs. One of the children that I observed had just recently started at the setting and was from an eastern European heritage. The setting had not been working with the family for long. Normally they would ask parents for key words in the child's language that they could use to try and help with communication, however, this had not yet happened. The parent had specifically asked that staff use English with the child. However, he seemed very confused by what was going on around him and did seem to relate better with one member of staff who was using Makaton. Without the consistency of this approach across the setting with each member of staff using it and acknowledging the benefits of it, its effectiveness may not be as advantageous as it could be. It is also prudent to note here that some parents are wary of signing as they feel that their children need to talk not use signs. However, in Makaton signs, symbols and language should be used together thus giving the child a pictorial clue to words.

Baldock (2010) suggests that sometimes it is important for one particular member of the team to take on the responsibility of augmenting cultural diversity in the setting. More recently in some areas of the country a role similar to that of a special educational needs co-ordinator (SENCO) has been introduced to settings, which does just this. According to Baldock (2010) the acronym ENCO stands for equalities named co-ordinator and their role is specifically to ensure that practitioners working in settings:

- ensure that resources represent many cultures;

- support children and families who may be using English as an additional language;

- ensure that legislation, policies and procedures are up to date; and

- self-evaluate and reflect on how multicultural the setting is.

While reporting on the need for measures such as this, Fisher (cited in Pitman 2015) states that 'people are not prepared enough for difference. The challenge is preparing people for living with difference. The opportunity is to turn diversity into an asset' (p. 4).

In areas of the country where these roles were introduced, training was provided for settings to ensure that staff were up to date with what was expected of them and ENCOs were utilised to help bridge some of the dilemmas that have already been discussed throughout this chapter. Baldock (2010) likewise discusses the need for all settings to represent diversity through their activities and resources, suggesting that good practice includes:

- posters that reflect diversity;

- treasure baskets and heuristic play;

- craft activities that reflect the diversity of cultures, especially if art from different parts of the world are included;

- painting activities that encourage children to mix paint and discuss how they are different (for example, see Figure 6.1, a piece of art painted by a child aged 4. She has been encouraged to think about how she is different from others in a very positive way. These activities can go a long way to encourage children to focus on difference in a very positive way);

- home corners that use different cooking instruments from around the world;

- food brought in from other cultures for children to taste, such as pizza, pasta, curry and stir-fries;

- pieces of fabric that can be used for children to dress up in rather than relying on dressing up clothes that represent characters from TV programmes.

Look carefully at books in your setting – how many of them represent multicultural Britain or are they in the main, related to white children? I remember when I was in Ghana a few years ago. I was reading stories to some children in a group and the book was related to Old Macdonald's farm. The children quickly became bored, despite my efforts to ensure that the sounds of the animals were authentic. It was not until I reflected on this situation that I realised there are no farms like Old Macdonald's in Ghana and I suspect that is why the children lost interest. The books need to reflect the everyday worlds of all children.

Treasure baskets and heuristic play activities both inside and out can inspire children to learn and can break down barriers of parents who do not quite understand the 'Western' fixation with toys. All of these activities will help children to see that people have different circumstances and live different and exciting lives.

Books for children

Browne, E. (1994) *Handa's Surprise*. London: Walker Books.

Cousins, L. (2011) *I'm the Best*. London: Walker Books.

Dawalt, D. (2016) *The Day the Crayons Came Home*. London: Harper Collins.

Hoffman, M. and Binch, C. (1991) *Amazing Grace*. London: Frances Lincoln Children's Books.

McKee, D. (1989) *Elmer*. London: Andersen Press.

Meek, A. and Massinin, S. (2005) *I'm Special, I'm Me!* London: Little Tiger Press.

Robert, N. and Adl, S. (2009) *Ramadan Moon*. London: Frances Lincoln Children's Books.

Conclusion

This chapter has discussed differences in people's view in relation to integration and inclusion, recognising it as a human right that all children should be respected and their culture and heritage celebrated. It has postulated on the need for a whole-team approach in order to ensure that consistent messages are given to all involved in the setting. The role of reflective practice has been disseminated and compared with the EYFS planning cycle and recognised as a useful tool for practitioners especially in relation to discussion around inclusion and diversity issues. Finally, suggestions have been made as to different practices and resources that can be used in settings.

The next chapter will consider the political and theoretical background of cultural diversity in early years practice.

Points to consider

- If you were trying to answer the question 'What is inclusion?' how would you respond? Try and come up with a paragraph of writing that sets out your particular view of inclusion.

- How does your setting view the inclusion of children from different cultures? Do you come from a monocultural area that feels that it does not need to represent other cultures? If so, how might you go about discussing this openly with your colleagues who may have different views to you?

- If you carried out an audit of the resources in your setting would they be representative of all cultures or predominantly just one? How might you start to address these issues?

- If you were trying to encourage young children to think about difference positively how might you plan activities around this?

Further reading

Kolb, D.A. (1984) *Experiential Learning*. New Jersey: Prentice Hall.

Early Education (2012) *Development Matters in the Early Years Foundation Stage*. London. www.early-education.org.uk/development-matters.

www.communicationpassports.org.uk/resources/References.

www.makaton.org.

wetalkmakaton.org.

References

Aboud, F.E., Tredoux, C., Tropp, L., Spears-Brown, R., Niens, C., Noor, U. and Noriaini, M. (2012) Interventions to reduce prejudice and enhance inclusion and respect for ethnic differences in early childhood: A systematic review. *Developmental Review* 32: 307–336.

Allan, J. (2008) *Rethinking Inclusion: The Philosophers of Difference in Practice*. Dordrecht: Springer.

Araujo, L. and Strasser, J. (2003) Confronting prejudice in the early childhood classroom. *Kappa Delta Pi Record* 39(4): 178–182.

Baldock, P. (2010) *Understanding Cultural Diversity in the Early Years*. London: Sage.

Beneke, M. and Cheatham, G.A. (2015) Speaking up for African American English: Equity and inclusion in early childhood settings. *Early Childhood Education* 43: 127–134.

Brookfield, S. (2006) *The Skilful Teacher on Technique, Trust and Responsiveness in the Classroom*. San Francisco, CA: Jossey-Bass.

Centre for Studies on Inclusive Education (2004) *Index for Inclusion: Developing Participation and Play in Early Years and Childcare*. Bristol. CSIE.

Corbett, J. (2001) *Supporting Inclusive Education: A Connective Pedagogy*. London: Falmer.

Department for Children, Schools and Families (2008) *Early Years Foundation Stage*. Nottingham: DCSF.

Devarakonda, C. (2013) *Diversity and Inclusion in Early Childhood: An Introduction*. London: Sage.

Early Education (2012) *Development Matters in the Early Years Foundation Stage*. London: Early Education.

Fisher, T. (2015) Helping every child succeed. *Early Education Journal* 75.

Gramelt, K. (2013) Diversity in early education: A German perspective. *Early Years* 33(1): 45–58.

Kay, J. (ed.) (2015) *Good Practice in the Early Years*. London: Continuum.

Kolb, D.A. (1984) *Experiential Learning*. New Jersey: Prentice Hall.

Levitas, R. (1998) *The Inclusive Society? Social Exclusion and New Labour*. Basingstoke: Macmillan.

The Makaton Charity (2016) What is Makaton? www.makaton.org.

Makaton.org. (n.d.) The Makaton vocabulary. www.makaton.org.

Millar, S. (2004) *Personal Communication Passports as a Way of Consulting and Representing Children with Communication Disabilities, to Ensure Consistent Care*. Edinburgh: University of Edinburgh.

Moss, P. (2007) Bringing politics into the nursery: Early childhood education as a democratic practice. *European Early Childhood Education Research Journal* 15(1): 5–20.

National Portage Association (2016) What is portage? www.portage.org.uk.

Nutbrown, C. and Clough, P. (2009) Citizenship and inclusion in the early years: Understanding and responding to children's perspectives on 'belonging'. *International Journal of Early Years Education* 3: 191–206.

Ofsted (2015) Ofsted examples of good practice in early years. www.gov.uk/government/collections/ofsted-examples-of-good-practice-in-early-years.

Pitman, J. (2015) Helping every child succeed. *Early Education Journal* 75: 4–6.

Rix, J. (2011) What's your attitude? Inclusion and early years settings. In Paige-Smith, A. and Craft, A. (eds) *Developing Reflective Practice in the Early Years* (2nd edition) (pp. 74–86). Buckingham: Open University Press.

Savage, K. (2015) Children, young people, inclusion and social policy. In Brodie, K. and Savage, K. (eds) *Inclusion and Early Years Practice* (pp. 1–17). Oxon: Routledge.

Save the Children (2009) Families and schools together. www.savethechildren.org.uk.

Unicef (1989) UN Convention on the Rights of the Child. www.unicef.org.uk.

The political context of cultural diversity

Introduction

This chapter will address some of the political context to cultural diversity focusing on two reports that were produced in the last century. The Plowden Report reviewed the role of education and suggested the need for all children to have access to early education after the age of 3. The Swann Report was written in response to a wave of immigration to the UK and the need for practitioners to carefully consider children from other cultures and their needs in terms of education. The UN Convention on the Rights of the Child introduced by Unicef in 1989 will receive some focus and critical analysis. The chapter will go on to discuss the history of the early years curriculum, from the Curriculum Guidance for the Foundation Stage that was introduced by the Qualifications and Curriculum Authority in 2000, to the present day. The evolving nature of the Early Years Foundation Stage (EYFS) (DFE 2014) will be considered, particularly focusing on what it has suggested in the past and now says about working with children from differing cultures and the recent launch of the 'fundamental British values' introduced to early years settings.

What is policy?

First, it is worth considering why policies are needed to support practice. There are many reasons why, but in the main they do the following (Levin 1997):

- guide and shape practice – the evolving nature of early years curriculum is an example of this. As new governments are elected, changes are often made to existing priorities depending on the political bias of the government in power;

- introduce new actions – the recent change to add British values to the curriculum is an indication of this;

- ensure that practice is fair and inclusive to all and also highlight new areas of concern for practitioners.

In terms of early years practice there are usually three layers of policy – first, that which is set at national level such as the EYFS and has been written by representatives chosen by the government. The second, at local level would include information handed down from local authorities. Finally, would be a settings policy and guidance on how national and local policies apply to individual settings.

It is worth pointing out at this stage that policies drawn up by government will constantly evolve and change, this is something that has been apparent through the EYFS since its inception in 2008. Policies reflect the views of government and the political party they represent, they also replicate what is going on in society and, as Moss (2003) asserts, are particularly based around the dominant culture of a country. Skeggs (1994, p. 77) also suggests that a country's 'social location and situatedness in the world' will influence how it speaks in terms of policy.

This can be an issue for families who come to the UK from other cultures whose experience of policy and education is very different to that of the UK. Tobin (2007) reports on research carried out with families and children from Mexico and the Caribbean when they came to early years settings in New York. Parents were becoming aggressive to practitioners and asking why children were encouraged to play when their parents wanted them to learn to 'write their names and know their numbers'. Staff felt threatened and their beliefs as educators were questioned. These kinds of issues can often create dilemmas in practice. Tobin suggests open dialogue is needed between practitioners and families in order that they can come to a joint decision regarding the curriculum on offer and discuss differences of views openly and in a sensitive way. This is why when there was significant immigration in the UK in the 1960s, reports were written and policy modified to ensure that the education of those coming from other countries was considered and appropriate adaptations made.

Multiculturalism in the UK

Issa and Hatt (2013) espouse the view that people have been coming to the UK from other countries for many thousands of years. They discuss the invasion of Roman times when people from other areas of the world settled here and point out that while some members of society view it as a new phenomenon, this is not the case. By the turn of the eighteenth century, Britain had become a 'multi-faith, multicultural country' with a mix of people with different faiths, nationalities and cultural experiences (Healey 2014). However, in the 1960s a large wave of people came to the UK particularly from Asia, Africa and the Caribbean islands in order to gain what they believed was a 'better life' for them and their families. In coming to the UK they brought with them very different identities and views in terms of education, faith, food and ways of living. For some this was seen as a threat to the 'British way of life', to many others it felt exciting and vibrant, and still does.

However, it is important to recognise that with these changes, educational policy needed to adapt. As children started going to school it was discovered that issues were arising for teachers in terms of their own perceptions of different communities. Bilingualism, faith and the different ways that groups of people lived needed to be represented within education. This led to the writing of new reports, postulating the view that the cultures of all should be celebrated and shared in order to support multiculturalism in the UK.

Case study 2.1

A few years ago I had the opportunity to visit early years settings in China and Hong Kong. Because of my interest in cultural diversity I was keen to go and to discover similarities and differences between the two countries.

I was surprised when arriving in China that some of the settings here are boarding schools. Often parents choose to send their children to what are seen as some of the 'better' early years settings while parents work full-time. Therefore the children stay at school all week, going home only at the weekends. The curriculum that is followed in the countries is also very different. I will admit that I expected it to be a lot more formal in the UK but I was pleasantly surprised. Children were involved with lots of art activities, music, drama, literacy and numeracy.

Sessions were quite prescriptive in comparison with the UK's idea of continuous provision and the staff were keen that children's work should look similar, compared to the UK where children are encouraged to individually create. The numbers of children attending the schools amazed me. Classes of 40–50 children were not uncommon and I enjoyed a demonstration of their music and movements sessions while visiting.

The following day was a Saturday and I was able to watch an English-speaking session with 3-year-olds. This totally blew my mind. Here 3-year-olds sat in a large circle of around 20 children and through rote learning discovered more about speaking English. If the children were not focused on the activities they would be turned around so that their faces were away from the remainder of the group. I was astonished and was therefore keen to ask the staff why it was that children were encouraged to learn English from such an early age. I was told that parents see the learning of the English language as a valuable skill in order for them to be equipped to live and work anywhere in the world when they grow up.

> From these experiences I learnt that as early years practition-
> ers we should never judge the practice of other countries or see
> it as less effective to how we do education in the UK.
>
> • What is your experience of working with children from other
>   cultures?
>
> • How might you start to work with families from other cultures
>   who may have different views about education than what is
>   offered in the UK?

The Plowden Report

The Plowden Report was written in 1967 when the Labour Government
led by Harold Wilson was in power. The Report was seen as an important
review of primary education in the UK. It postulated that the child should
be at the heart of the educational process and that children should be
seen as individuals rather than a homogenised group all needing the
same process of education. The Report was based on Piaget's (1962)
'cognitive view of development', which sets out the idea that children
develop in ages and stages, a theory that has been fiercely debated by
some, such as Sylva (1987) and Donaldson (1978). The Report did,
however, raise the idea that play is central to children's development
and it introduced the view that very young children should also be
educated. This was a new concept in UK history and set the starting
point for early years education as we know it today.

The Plowden Report dedicated an entire chapter to the 'children of
immigrants'. Much was said in the Report of the language gap and 'culture shock' that families were experiencing and the need to tackle this
within the education system. However, the need for teachers to address
such issues brought with it the view that 'teachers lack the knowledge
of the cultural traditions and family structures that lie behind children's
concepts and behaviour' (HMSO 1967, p. 45). The chapter concluded
that teachers should use differing cultures as an opportunity for teaching,

particularly in terms of geography and history of the world. This should therefore mean that all children will grow up to respect and appreciate other cultures and traditions. A view that is endorsed by Friendly (2007) who suggests that school can be a critical place for children to learn about tolerance of others, difference and diversity in an unbiased way.

The Swann Report: education for all

The Swann Report was written in 1985 during Margaret Thatcher's Conservative leadership and was a response to a review by the West Indian Community to the Commons Select Committee on Race Relations and Immigration that had been written in 1977. The Report discusses the assimilation approach to integration, which is a view of how a culture adopts the characteristics of other ethnic groups and how groups of people come to resemble one another. However, this was more in relation to how ethnic communities should come together and take on the white, Christian and English culture rather than white people assimilating the cultures of others.

The enquiry was requested in response to the poor attainment levels of children, particularly from West Indian communities. It is interesting to note that although the Report was written in 1977 it took eight years for it to be published. The Report highlighted the difficulties that families were experiencing and the effect that these had on a child's well-being and their ability to learn. Again, as with the Plowden Report, issues around language and 'culture shock' were highlighted. The Report discussed the view that rather than assimilating into 'white, Christian and English-speaking areas', a more 'planned and detailed education and social programme' was needed to ensure that a more 'culturally diverse society would be created'. Once again it was pointed out that the geographical and historical factors affecting cultures should be shared thus hoping that this would assist with community cohesion. The authors also highlighted that 'a climate should be created in schools in which colour and race are not divisive and that would give all indigenous children opportunities for personal development in their new environment' (HMSO 1985).

However, although this endorses more of an integrationist approach to cultural diversity, which respects cultures and supports the coming together and acceptance of all, as with the Plowden Report it says nothing about the need for white children to do the same in terms of discovering more about the cultures from which other children come.

The UN Convention on the Rights of the Child

The charity organisation Unicef established the Convention in 1989. It set out to be a complete statement of children's rights across the world. It adopts 54 articles that cover all aspects of a child's life and ensures that children worldwide have the same rights and entitlements. It has changed how children are thought of quite considerably. Before the statement, children were often seen as vulnerable and lacking a voice. The Convention changed the status of a child to being someone with a voice and an entitlement to have a say in all matters that affect them. All UN members except for the USA have signed up to the Convention and in 1992 it became law throughout the UK. It gives a global commitment to children's rights. It does, however, have its critics as it is said by some to support 'Western values' that may be inappropriate to children growing up in developing countries. As Stephens (1995, p. 32) observes, some critics of the Convention argue 'that its declaration of universal children's rights gives children the right to be remade in the image of adults and non-Western childhoods the right to be remade in Western forms'. Waldren and Kaminski (2012, p. 3) also state that the Convention has a tendency to 'clump children together irrespective of the culture and class' that they are growing up in.

The term 'Western childhoods' refers to those children growing up in the West. It does not focus on those growing up in what we know as developing countries, who may not have a roof over their heads, do not have free access to schools and some, in countries like India, China or Bangladesh, who are expected to work and bring home money to their families.

Cregan and Cuthbert (2014, p. 56) also have contrasting views about the Convention stating that 'Endowing children with rights that many are unable to exercise without adult intervention because of their age, capacity and access to resources is unfair'.

A closer examination of the individual articles begins to reveal how different interpretations are possible. For instance, Article 24 states that all children should have the right to access 'good quality health care, clean water, nutritious food and a clean environment so that children can stay healthy'. Yet in some areas of the world, water is not clean, there is little food and children live in abject poverty, despite the Convention setting out how richer countries should help poorer areas of the world.

Articles 28 and 29 point out the right for all children to access education. Article 30 specifically relates to children who may move to a different country to live and sets out:

> In those States in which ethnic, religious or linguistic minorities or persons of indigenous origin exist, a child belonging to such a minority or who is indigenous shall not be denied the right, in community with other members of his or her group, to enjoy his or her own culture.
>
> (Unicef 1989, p. 10)

So, in line with the Plowden and Swann Reports, children from other cultures have just as much right to education and to enjoy his or her culture in whatever country they live.

Reflection points

- Do you think it is fair that some children in the world have access to education whereas others have to spend their days working to bring money home to their families?

- Why are there so many inequalities in the world for children?

- Are inequalities in the developing world something that people in the developed world should be concerned about?

Early years curriculum

Under the leadership of Tony Blair between 1997 and 2007 and the introduction of New Labour there was a raft of changes made to early years provision across the country. The Curriculum Guidance for the Foundation Stage was introduced in 2000 in an effort to improve the quality of practice across all early years provisions available to families. In many areas of the country, schools built nurseries that offered part-time early years provision. This ensured that when children entered school at 5 years old they were better able to cope with its demands and were better acclimatised to the expectations of school. Prior to this, children would be sent to voluntarily run playgroups and preschools. As more women returned to work, non-maintained provision increased around the country through privately run nurseries. Childminding became more popular as childminders could offer one-to-one care at home, replicating the domestic situation for children. However, settings in the past were not governed by any particular curriculum. New Labour sought to address growing levels of poverty in the UK so Sure Start children's centres were introduced initially into the poorest areas of the country and then countrywide in order to encourage parents to work. These offered a range of multi-agency support and advice as well as high-quality early years provisions for families. One of the main purposes of children's centres was to ensure that parents from diverse communities were encouraged to engage with groups provided by the centres and to feel more included in the area over time. The launch of the Curriculum Guidance for the Foundation Stage was an attempt to offer standardised provision to young children across the UK while accepting that it may be delivered differently depending on the kind of provision accessed. What did this document promote in relation to the cultural diversity of young children? It was quick to point out that settings should:

- follow an inclusive ethos that all parents should be welcomed to the setting;

- ensure that no child should be excluded because of their ethnicity, faith, family background or ability;

- employ multilingual staff who represent the diversity of the community;

- display posters and resources to represent the cultures in the community;

- encourage early years practitioners to celebrate the life experiences of all families and accept the experiences, interests, skills and knowledge of all children.

Birth to Three Matters

In 2005, a new curriculum was developed by Sure Start in order to meet and address the many expanding childcare places. Birth to Three Matters was developed to ensure that children were encouraged to be competent learners from birth. This recognised that more parents were leaving their children in early years settings because they were at work, and it was seen as a drive to ensure quality provision for the youngest children whose needs were not being met by the Curriculum Guidance for the Foundation Stage. The framework offered settings the opportunity to recognise the 'holistic nature of development and learning'. It encouraged staff to 'identify characteristics of children in settings' and to plan accordingly while also celebrating the unique nature and culture of each child.

Early Years Foundation Stage (EYFS)

In 2008, the government combined the Curriculum Guidance for the Foundation Stage, Birth to Three and the National Standards for Under 8s Daycare and Childminding and developed the Early Years Foundation Stage. This new amalgamated policy was to be used for all children aged 0–5. It introduced into settings for the first time the principle of the 'unique child', which suggests that 'every child is a competent learner from birth who can be resilient, capable, confident and self assured' (DCSF 2008, p. 5).

The document goes on to state that the diverse needs of children should be celebrated and also introduced the requirement that practitioners should offer 'personalised learning' that promotes 'positive attitudes' to diversity and difference in all children (DFES 2008, p. 6). It goes on to declare that practitioners must plan for the needs of children from varying cultures and that issues of discrimination must be challenged. As Plowden had suggested back in 1967, the document makes the case that the best way for young children to develop and learn is through well-planned play that is not only adult led but can be instigated and led by children themselves. The policy, as with the previous Curriculum Guidance for the Foundation Stage (DFEE/QCA 2000) stressed the importance of ensuring that the diversity of children and communities is respected and celebrated and ensures that no family should be discriminated against.

The document also offers a challenge to practitioners that they should ensure that their own development of knowledge around other cultures remains up to date. They are also required to actively promote anti-discriminatory practice as well as maintaining a respectful dialogue between parents and carers, accepting that parents are a child's first educator.

There is also acceptance of families' spiritual belief systems within the curriculum. This is an area of life that is, I feel, rarely mentioned in settings unless there is a festival approaching. For certain communities, faith is an integral part of their lives and while in the UK church numbers are declining (Faith Survey 2012), in other types of Christianity and other beliefs the living out of faith is a daily expression of who they are. This needs to be accepted by practitioners whether or not they themselves are believers. This can greatly affect a child's identity, as we shall see when we move on to the next chapter, and can be an important aspect of a child's life. It saddens me when settings portray Christmas as being about Father Christmas and Easter relating to eggs and bunnies. The festivity of Diwali, which is often celebrated around bonfire night, tends to be combined and activities relating to light are promoted. When Eid is being celebrated it is often just portrayed as a time of festivity and parties, which it is, but it is also about so much more than this. It is not about trying to convert families into any one particular faith group but about recognising that we live in a culturally diverse community and world.

Reflection points

- Have you ever considered that families/children attending your setting may follow certain faith groups in their homes?

- How are different celebrations and festivities celebrated in your setting?

- What more could you do in your setting to ensure that all celebrations are considered?

In 2010 the Conservative and Liberal Democrat coalition government under the leadership of David Cameron requested a review of the EYFS as it was felt to be too bureaucratic and that practitioners were confused by the complexity of the original document. Dr Clare Tickell, a Doctor of Law at Bristol University, chaired the review. She acknowledged the importance of the EYFS but concluded that it was cumbersome and repetitive in parts. She committed to the document remaining mandatory for all settings to use but recommended that there should be greater assessment in terms of what children can do. The review requested that the current EYFS should be scaled down in order to make it a more workable document for practitioners. Some of the requirements of the review are as follows:

- The role of parents is accepted and celebrated and settings need to ensure that they demonstrate closer working relationships with families.

- Children should be encouraged to develop their communication skills, which are responsive to the child's interests, home language and wider development.

- Children who are falling behind in areas of their development should be able to access different agencies more swiftly.

- Bilingualism should be recognised as being an asset to children, and parents should encourage use of their home language both at home and in settings. However, children should have good communication skills in English, as they will be particularly needed when children enter Key Stage 1 of the education system.

Ang (2010) has written about elements of cultural diversity that are encapsulated in the EYFS. She draws on the novel *Anita and Me*, written by Meera Syal about her experiences of coming to the UK from the Punjab. Syal talks about the first year that she was in the UK and how she felt alienated when she went into school. In the book she addresses the sadness she felt when all her friends were enjoying Christmas but there was no mention of the Diwali festival celebrated by Hindus, which her and her family were celebrating. Ang (2010) draws a parallel here between Syal's experience and the EYFS, suggesting that it does not focus on cultural diversity enough. She goes on to discuss how the document addresses issues relating to social justice, equality and the need to celebrate the festivities of cultural groups and communities but suggests that it gives an 'elitist notion of culture' (p. 45), arguing that the British culture is that which is extolled in the main throughout the document. Ang (2010) goes on to state that it is not in line with the 'constantly evolving' population in the UK and the 'increasing numbers of children who are bi racial or from mixed heritages' (p. 43). Ang (2010, p. 48) challenges the government to consider more those children that come from 'linguistically and culturally diverse communities' to ensure that early years provision is appropriate for the learning and development of all children. She also discusses the fact that the EYFS is only written in English, which could be a challenge for practitioners for whom English is their second language. Finally, Ang (2010) suggests that the EYFS 'falls short' of addressing inclusive learning and teaching as it gives no indication of what this is, how it might be implemented and presented by practitioners and furthermore how it accepts the wider view of parents from different communities who might have a different view of education.

EYFS (2014)

In 2014 the new EYFS was launched by the Department for Education. This document addresses the many changes suggested through the Tickell Review and adds that one of the important things that practitioners need to do is to enable children to be 'school ready'. Although the principles continue to extol the concept of the unique child, the emphasis around cultural diversity seems to have changed. The first EYFS was probably not quite the document that Ang (2010) aspired to but it does at least recognise that the UK is an ever-evolving society where families from across the world choose to come and live and that is celebrated by practitioners. However, the caveat around bilingualism that Tickell recommends does not really suggest that Dr Tickell necessarily celebrates the diversity of the UK. Rather, it suggests that bilingualism in families is acceptable up to the age of 6, but then the child has to become completely literate in English. As we shall see later on in the book, bilingualism does not work like this and so there may be a worry that we may be setting children up to fail early on in their school careers.

Reflection points

- Do you feel that the EYFS meets the needs of all children?

- Are there certain groups of children that the EYFS does not seem to mention?

- How good is the EYFS at supporting practitioners in meeting the needs of all children?

Prevent Duty

In June 2015 the Conservative government unveiled its plans, in order to meet the requirements of the Prevent Duty. The Education Secretary at the time, Nicky Morgan, announced plans to embed British values into current practice. This was in order to reduce misinterpretation and confusion around fundamentalism and extremist views. It was reported that any settings that were seen to be advocating certain extremist views would have their early education funding removed. British values ensure that children are taught about democracy and their entitlement to have views and for those views to be listened to and accepted. It extols the need for children to understand that rules matter and that their behaviour can affect how these rules are dealt with – helping children to learn right from wrong. Finally, the values discuss the need for mutual respect and tolerance of all faiths, cultures and races while ensuring that children learn positively about the differences between certain groups. It goes on to excel the need for practitioners to 'promote diverse attitudes and challenge stereotypes' while valuing the diversity of children's experiences.

However, there have been criticisms of the need for this to be done in early years settings. It was reported by many other leaders of early years groups such as the Preschool Learning Alliance and the National Day Nurseries Association that settings are already doing this, as many of these suggested actions are already required through the EYFS document. It is suggested that actions like these need to be done in an age-appropriate way and that this may be quite an extreme reaction to radicalisation. Perhaps it is an issue that practitioners need to be notified about but caution should also be observed. It is a minority of people who do become radicalised and for the majority of early years settings it is not an issue. However, it is worrying when you hear of situations when staff in a setting had been concerned about something that had arisen in the classroom but when they delved a little deeper it was more about their lack of knowledge of different cultures. This once again suggests the need for practitioners to continue to update their knowledge of all cultures through well-developed inclusive training.

EYFS (2015)

In September 2017 the Department for Education produced another updated EYFS. Here we see the acceptance that all children are individuals and that child development should be about both the biological and cultural aspects of the child, however, far more emphasis is placed on assessment in this document. It discusses the need for children to be assessed *in English* at the end of the EYFS; this notes down areas that they excel or have a weakness in. The new document strongly advocates the need for children to be adept in communicating with others and points out that this is a central requirement in life. It discusses the need for bilingual practitioners to support parents' understanding of bilingualism and to support practitioners to make accurate assessment of the language of children. However, the document does extol the need for children to continue to use their home language alongside English as well as the environment reflecting the cultural and linguistic heritage within the community. The document continues to acknowledge that parents from other cultures may have differing views on the education system in the UK and that this may make a difference to their assessment through the EYFS. For instance, a child who may have come with their professional parents to the UK from India may have been brought up to count by rote and attempt to read earlier on than their English-born counterparts, which could mean that they are quite fluent in their ability to count but may not truly understand what numbers mean. The document continues to suggest that 'Children will be able to demonstrate their attainment best when opportunities such as role play, cookery, celebrations, visits to special places or events are linked to their cultural experience' (DfE 2017).

The document suggests that through their play and exploration children should be able to make sense of their world and value the diversity of society, and that through practitioners' involvement with parents they too may learn how families live and work, which can then have a bearing on their understanding of different communities.

All of this is, however, easier to determine if your setting is in a culturally diverse area but not quite so easy, but just as important, if you work in a very monocultural area. The same policy requirements apply wherever in the country you live and work, so it is important that it should be everyday practice in all settings.

Case study 2.2

I recently went out to Ghana with a group of undergraduate students. Ghana is now seen as one of the developing countries of Africa but there are still large areas of the country where families live in abject poverty and where children are not able to go to school, particularly girls. The government was trying to implement a new early years curriculum that highlighted the need for children to learn through play. Prior to this the syllabus was very much based around children learning to read, write and do numeracy activities. The conference was attended by around 250 people and was a great success. Following on from this the students went to placements in early years settings represented at the conference in order to try and support staff with activities around play. This was not without its issues. Staff were not easily persuaded that children could necessarily learn through play and old habits and routines were hard to break.

During the visit we spent the weekends going to different areas of the country where we saw evidence of the large-scale poverty, which is still apparent in the country. I found myself feeling that if I was a parent living in Ghana I could quite understand why families want their children to learn to read and write as early as possible – it could be seen to be a way out of poverty. My views about the play-led curriculum completely changed after this.

This is evidence of where a developing country has different issues to those that we see in the UK.

Reflection

- Is it right for us to impose a similar curriculum in a country where learning to read and write can help children and families to come out of poverty?

Conclusion

This chapter has discussed some of the historical and political context to cultural diversity. It has sought to critique the curriculum while challenging the reader to not only consider their own cultural views but also to think about policy in the national and international forum. It has discussed in depth the evolving nature of the curriculum in the UK and suggested that at times this does not particularly reflect the fluid nature of communities in the UK. The next chapter will focus on the theoretical perspective of cultural diversity.

Points to consider

- How much are practitioners in your setting made aware of changes to early years policies that may relate to cultural diversity?

- Does your setting have a policy that relates to cultural diversity? If so, how are practitioners made aware of this and what it says?

- How do you ensure that you find out from parents about their culture and any belief system they may follow?

- How do you discover the expectations of parents around children's learning and how this may happen?

Further reading

Baldock, P., Fitzgerald, D. and Kay, J. (2013) *Understanding Early Years Policy* (3rd edition). London: Sage.

Nursery World (2015) Nurseries must teach 'British values' or lose their funding. www.nurseryworld.co.uk.

Unicef (1989) *The United Nations Convention on the Rights of the Child*. London: Unicef.

References

Ang, L. (2010) Critical perspectives on cultural diversity in early childhood: Building an inclusive curriculum and provision. *Early Years: An International Research Journal* 30(1): 41–52.

Cregan, K. and Cuthbert, D. (2014) *Global Childhoods: Issues and Debates*. London: Sage.

Department for Children, Schools and Families (DCSF) (2008) *Practice Guidance for the Early Years Foundation Stage*. Nottingham: DCSF.

Department for Education (DFE) (2014) Early Years (Under 5s) Foundation Stage Framework (EYFS). www.gov.uk/government/publications/early-years-foundation-stage-framework--2.

DFE (2017) Early Years (Under 5s) Foundation Stage Framework (EYFS). www.gov.uk/government/publications/early-years-foundation-stage-framework--2.

DFEE/QCA (2000) *Curriculum Guidance for the Foundation Stage*. Hertfordshire: DFEE.

Donaldson, M. (1978) *Children's Minds*. London: Harper Collins.

The Faith Survey (2012) Christianity in the UK. https://faithsurvey.co.uk/uk-christianity.html.

Friendly, M. (2007) How ECEC programmes contribute to social inclusion in diverse societies. *Early Childhood Matters* 108: 11–14. The Netherlands: Bernard van Leer Publications.

Healey, J. (2014) The real history of multicultural Britain. https://thesocialhistorian.wordpress.com/2014/10/02/the-real-history-of-multicultural-britain/.

Her Majesty's Stationery Office (HMSO) (1967) *The Plowden Report: Children and Their Primary Schools*. London: HMSO.

HMSO (1985) *The Swann Report: Education for All*. London: HMSO.

Issa, T. and Hatt, A. (2013) *Language, Culture and Identity in the Early Years*. London: Bloomsbury.

Levin, P. (1997) *Making Social Policy: The Mechanisms of Government and Politics to Investigate Them*. Buckingham: Open University Press.

Moss, P. (2003) 'Getting beyond childcare: Reflections on recent policy and future possibilities'. In Brannen, J. and Moss, P. (eds) *Rethinking Children's Care* (pp. 1–21). Buckingham: Open University Press.

Piaget, J. (1962) *Play, Dreams, and Imitation in Childhood.* New York: W.W. Norton.

Skeggs, B. (1994) *The Constraints of Neutrality: The 1988 Education Reform Act and Feminist Research.* London: The Falmer Press.

Stephens, S. (1995) Introduction: Children and the politics of culture. In Stephens, S. (ed.) *Children and the Politics of Culture* (pp. 3–48). New Jersey: Princeton.

Sure Start (2005) *Birth to Three Matters.* www.foundationyears.org.uk/wp-content.

Sylva, Kathy (1987) Plowden: History and prospect. *Oxford Review of Education* 13(1): 3–11.

Tickell, C. (2011) *The Early Years: Foundations for Life, Health and Learning: An Independent Report on the Early Years Foundation Stage to Her Majesty's Government.* www.education.gov.uk.

Tobin, J. (2007) Entering into dialogue with immigrant parents. *Early Childhood Matters* 108: 33–38. The Netherlands: Bernard van Leer Publications.

Unicef (1989) *The United Nations Convention on the Rights of the Child.* London: Unicef.

Waldren, J. and Kaminski, I. (eds) (2012) *Learning from the Children: Childhood, Culture and Identity in a Changing World.* Oxford: Berghahn Books.

How does theory relate to cultural diversity?

3

Introduction

This chapter will focus on some of the theories around cultural diversity. The information should be seen as an introduction to views that will be discussed in more depth in subsequent chapters. It is intended to give 'a glimpse' to certain theoretical viewpoints. Further reading would be needed to fully understand the concepts and principles within these theories.

The views of Jerome Bruner, Urie Bronfenbrenner, Barbara Rogoff and Liz Brooker will be considered. Before these theories are discussed, it is important to consider that many of the child development theories that are popular today come from the Westernised world. They originate from Europe, Australia, Canada and the United States of America. However, only 18 per cent of children living in the world populate these areas. Smidt (2006, p. 27) suggests that 'a notion of universality' has occurred that encourages practitioners to think that all children across the world develop in the same way. Although this may be true physically, the way that children are brought up and live their lives, I would suggest, may be very different.

Jerome Bruner

Gray and Macblain (2015) record that Bruner was born in the US in 1915, and died in June 2016. Bruner worked with the US army before becoming an academic at Harvard University. His theory about how children learn relates to the social-constructivism field of child development. This suggests that children not only learn through their cognitive/mental aptitudes but also from people, society and their environment. Bruner places emphasis on the fact that the cultural element of a family is an important part of the way that children are brought up and forms the foundation stone of their lives. He values the role of the adult, whether that is someone in the child's family, a teacher/practitioner or an elder in the community. Bruner views all of these as being an essential aspect of a child's learning.

As was noted in the previous chapter, it is important to understand that child development cannot be considered in a vacuum – it often relates to the context of what is going on in the world at the time that theorists are carrying out their research. Bruner's work was related very closely to the social and economic changes going on in the US around race in the early 1950s. At this time children from different cultures and backgrounds were being segregated in American schools and Korea was about to go to war in Vietnam. Bruner emphasised the role of culture in helping children to shape their thinking and experience and also questioned some of the underlying policy and decision makers in education at that time. He believed that previous child development studies had focused too much on the nature of what a child is asked to do and there was 'too little focus on the dynamic qualities the child brought to the tasks in order to solve them' (Brown 1975, p. 74).

Bruner viewed learning as something that takes place when a child is actively involved in a task, whether that is playing, exploring how something works or being in a new environment. He was more fascinated by the way that children develop strategies and processes to learn and how these experiences aid them. Importantly Bruner was interested in how certain stimuli are presented and how these help children to learn. He believed that children learn through three ways:

- The *enactive* mode – concerned with actions.

- The *iconic* mode – concerned with images.

- The *symbolic* mode – concerned with symbols such as words and language.

Bruner also placed great emphasis on the way that adults can help children to learn, viewing them as instruments who share their knowledge of both the level of a child's development and also the way that the child prefers to learn. Therefore the adult is able to extend the child's learning in the way that will best suit them.

Scaffolding

One of Bruner's most popular concepts is that of scaffolding. This is where adults or peers assist children in learning new skills, and it refers to the way that children are supported in this process. Just as a scaffold helps a building to stay up when work is being carried out on it, scaffolding relates to the framework of support an adult gives to a child by breaking learning down while supporting the child through each part of their learning until they are able to complete it in its entirety independently. So, for example, you might be supporting a toddler to complete an inset jigsaw puzzle. To begin with you might point to the space where the piece needs to be and praise the child enthusiastically when they put the piece in the correct hole. As the child becomes more proficient, the support and praise of the adult is lessened until the child is able to complete the puzzle unsupported. Practitioners will recognise this concept as being absolutely central to their role in an early years setting.

The spiral curriculum

Rather than viewing development as Piaget (1959) did – in linear stages that children meet at certain ages – Bruner saw development as being integrated, suggesting that learning should happen in a spiral. He is well known for developing the notion of the 'spiral curriculum'. This is when concepts are introduced to children time and time again but at different stages in their learning. To begin with, a very young baby will be stretching and moving, they will be finding out what their actions can do and then latterly they will begin to realise that they can have an impact on toys by pushing them or dropping them. This is evidence of Bruner's enactive mode. As the child is able to hold more they can be encouraged to carry out activities that may support them with their handwriting. Practitioners will encourage this in many different ways. The child will move from using a palmar, full-handed grip as they grow to be able to use a tripod grip, which means that they can hold a pencil correctly. Other activities such as those involving sand or cornflour paste encourage children to make shapes with their fingers or twigs and paint brushes. This is a demonstration of how the enactive mode then moves into the iconic mode as children start to recognise the images they have made in the mixture, and then when the child begins to put pen to paper and make marks, the symbolic mode is represented. The role of the adult is crucial here to ensure that they know the child well enough to be able to scaffold activities within the child's level of development. The child will then move on to being able to write, therefore representing the symbolic mode.

Bruner viewed settings and schools as being one part of a child's knowledge but certainly not the whole, thus recognising the wider contexts of the impact that culture, society and the environment can have on children's learning. He talks of 'implicit cultural practices' (Tobin, Hsueh and Karasawa 2009, p. 19), which are not taught in schools but that are 'taken-for-granted practices that emerge from embedded cultural beliefs that relate to how children learn and teachers teach' (Bruner 1996, p. 46)

A different view is suggested by Hyun (cited in Tobin et al. 2009, p. 262), who views schools as being somewhere that children from all cultures can come together and engage in 'critical and ethical reflection about what it means to belong to different cultures'.

Language

Bruner places great importance on the role of language in a child's world. He views language as being the way that children ask for things, talk through their actions and the way that they problem solve and socialise with others. Bruner viewed practitioners and adults as being a child's 'Language Acquisition Support System' (LASS). As early years practitioners, you will recognise the importance of communication skills to a child's development. Bruner views practitioners as vital instruments to help children communicate. Adults are able to interpret the body language that babies use. Then through encouragement and by extending children's linguistic capabilities, practitioners urge children to discuss activities that they are taking part in. It is widely acknowledged that children who struggle using language may grow up to be children who struggle with later elements of their learning. Bruner saw language as 'enabling children to internally represent their learning in sophisticated ways' (Gray and Macblain 2015, p. 137). This places importance on encouraging children to use their home language in settings to communicate, as well as having bilingual staff available to assist children who may be learning more than one language.

Reflection points

- Have you ever considered Bruner's modes of development before? How do they relate to the children that you are currently working with?

- Do you see yourself as Bruner does in terms of supporting children's language development?

- How do you ensure that you and your colleagues scaffold children's learning?

Urie Bronfenbrenner

Gray and Macblain (2015) note that Urie Bronfenbrenner was born in Russia in 1917, he then moved with his family to the US at the age of 6. After winning a scholarship to university he studied psychology.

Then, like Bruner, he went to serve in the army as a psychologist. In common with Bruner, Bronfenbrenner believed that children constantly change and that life experiences as well as cultural heritage have an impact on their lives and their learning. This theory is known as the ecological systems theory.

Bronfenbrenner was the co-founder of the Head Start programme in the US – this is similar to Sure Start programmes in the UK, which were first developed to support families living in deprived areas and subsequently were situated across the country. Bronfenbrenner noticed that there was less academic achievement in children growing up in these deprived areas than their counterparts living in more affluent areas of the country. In the US these programmes have been going since 1995 and, although they have changed slightly in their delivery, they are still seen as being central to the academic achievement of many children.

Bronfenbrenner views children as being 'unique individuals' – a term also reflected in the EYFS (DCSF 2008). According to Boyatzis (1998), Bronfenbrenner views development occurring 'within a multitude of different but nested contexts', which he believes have a direct impact on a child's learning and development. As with Bruner, Bronfenbrenner also emphasises the view of the environment as being an important part of a child's life. Bronfenbrenner's ecological systems theory takes the form of four concentric circles placed within each other: the microsystem, mesosystem, exosystem and macrosystem. Gray and Macblain (2015) suggest that a similar way to view this theory is as a set of Russian dolls with the smallest being at the centre.

Microsystem

The child is the central tenet of Bronfenbrenner's theory. Inside the first circle, sit the parents, siblings and peers that the child has regular contact with. The community and neighbourhood where the family lives are also included centrally, as are practitioners who support the child and family. In earlier illustrations of this theory, the faith system that the child may grow up in is significant. This may be because of the time that Bronfenbrenner's theory was written and the relevance of the church during that time. It may seem unusual to those of us living in the Western world where religion is not always seen as being as important, but in many parts of the world faith is a vital element, and so it is my view that this aspect should not be removed.

Mesosystem

The next layer of the systems theory relates to areas of life that the child is directly involved in, so it might be the home, place of worship, neighbourhood and setting. The theory suggests that these elements are not static but that the microsystem relates with the mesosystem. So the relationship that the family has with all of these elements is constantly evolving and changing. This can be observed when a child starts school and new relationships are built up within the school environment. Suddenly parents may feel that they have less say over their child's upbringing. Children make new friends and are required to conform to new ways of being which are asserted by teachers rather than their parents.

Exosystem

The next layer of the theory discusses the relevance of school governors, local government, the parents' workplace, mass media and local industry and again relates to relationships that this layer has with the others. An example of this would be the government's policy to extend the amount of free childcare for all parents of 3- and 4-year-olds (Gov. UK 2015). Here we see that in providing this, local authorities will need to ensure that there are an acceptable number of childcare places available.

However, in some cultures it is not customary for parents to send their children to childcare. Girls are encouraged to stay behind and help to care for their siblings, and so it may only be boys who benefit from early childcare (Nganga 2009). In some black and minority ethnic communities it is more traditional for children to be cared for by members of their extended family (Sure Start 2004). Kenner *et al.* (2007) relay how, in Bengali culture and communities, grandparents are considered to play a major role in children's education. So we should never assume that people coming to the UK will automatically want to put their children into early years settings.

Macrosystem

The final layer of the theory focuses on the cultures, faith, legal and societal institutions as well as the dominant beliefs and ideologies that pervade society. If we take the example of the Childcare Bill, one of the dominant principles that this promotes is that women should have the right to work so therefore they need affordable childcare that will facilitate this. However, as we saw previously, this may not be the custom with all communities where the priority may be for women to stay at home to bring up their children.

The fact that people's dominant belief systems and ideologies may differ also needs consideration. It can no longer be assumed that because we all live in the same country that all communities share a common set of beliefs, values and history. Different faith groups may raise their children differently and may have different ideologies around childcare to others.

Case study 3.1

Rukaiya is 6 years old and has just moved from Reception to Year 1 at school. She is the youngest child in a family of five. She has two older brothers one of which attends Year 2 of the same school. The family live very near to the school and are important people in the local community. They are also very supportive of their children and their father is on the board of governors.

Rukaiya settled into school very quickly and enjoys all elements of her school life; one of her favourite things is to sing.

The school has a large choir, which they invite children to join and that meets one day a week after school. Rukaiya is desperate to join, however all children in the family attend the Madrasa at the local mosque each day after school.

A Madrasa is a place where Muslim children go to learn about their faith, to read the Koran and to receive religious education. This is a very important element of the children's faith.

Rukaiya recognises the importance of the Madrasa in her life but she asks her family if she could miss this just for one day each week so that she can join the choir. Her parents talked to the leader of the choir and it is agreed that she can join the choir and miss the Madrasa for one day a week.

Reflection

- If you had a family in your setting whose child was facing a similar dilemma how would you try to deal with the situation?

- How well do you work with other 'institutions' in your community to ensure that there is a collective understanding of each other's roles and how you can work together to support families?

Representation of Bronfenbrenner's theory

There have been many diagrams illustrating this theory over the years: for example, Russian dolls and concentric circles and some may include arrows to demonstrate the relationships between each layer. However, by using circles with unbroken lines, I am not sure that this correctly displays the relationships that each layer has with the others, a view consolidated by Rogoff (2003), who believes that diagrams need to represent the view that 'cultural and personal processes create each other' (p. 49). Instead of concentric circles, I would rather view

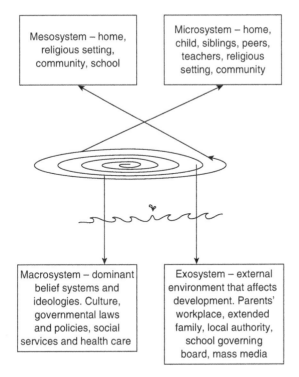

Figure 3.1 Representation of Urie Bronfenbrenner's theory

Bronfenbrenner's theory as ripples within a pool. When a pebble is thrown into a pool it creates ripples that move in relationship with one another, they quickly evolve from one circle to two, three and maybe four ripples. For me this better illustrates Bronfenbrenner's ecological systems theory (see Figure 3.1). Boyatzsis (1998) stresses the need for educators to understand the interwovenness of development and culture in a child's life.

Barbara Rogoff

Another theorist who firmly recognises the role of culture in a child's life is Barbara Rogoff. An American educator born in the US in

1950, she has spent much of her working life researching how different cultures evolve and live. Like Bruner, her theories fall into the social constructivist area of work whereby children learn not just from their cognitive abilities but also from society and their environments. However, Rogoff moves the theory on slightly by recognising that a family's culture and belief system are vital elements of their lives and that practitioners need to take these into consideration when working with them.

Rogoff recognises that children across the world are different and so have different opportunities to live, be educated and be part of their communities and society. She goes on to endorse the view that ideas about childhood should never be generalised and practitioners should never make assumptions about the way that children are brought up and live. Her theory therefore follows the sociocultural view of childhood that, rather than viewing children as a homogenous group, their different cultures should be viewed as being 'exciting, informing and enlightening' (Barr and Borkett 2015, p. 282). Rogoff (2003) states that those of us from the West should not make 'unquestioned assumptions stemming from our own community practices' (p. 11) but instead should take note of the cultural practices that are all around us and learn from these. One way of doing this may be through travelling to other places and acknowledging and engaging with difference both in the way that groups of people live and the way that they bring up their children. However, you do not need to go abroad to witness this, often moving to another area of a city can help you to acknowledge that people live very differently.

During my life I have moved within the UK three times. In each area I have witnessed people acknowledging distinct traditions, speaking numerous dialects and living their lives similarly yet differently. Problems arise, however, when people view their ways of life as being superior to others. A word of caution from Waldren and Kaminski (2012) suggests that childhood should never be 'normalised' as it always depends on society, culture and the historic period of the time. However, Rogoff (2003) suggests that to really understand a culture one needs to immerse oneself in it.

A few years ago while carrying out some research that investigated the views of parents relating to play (see Chapter 1), I was interviewing a grandmother and her granddaughter and the only place where the research could be carried out was the grandmother's fabric shop. This lay right in the heart of the community on the main road where there was an abundance of shops selling different foods from around the world. As many Asian families make their own clothes and sewing is a skill that is often handed down the generations, the shop was always busy. I set up my microphone and started to ask the questions. No sooner had I asked my first question than a customer came into the shop, this continued to happen throughout the interview. However, rather than being frustrated that the interview had taken longer than I had hoped, I found the experience fascinating. Not only had I discovered a lot about both family members' views of play, I also had the experience of being immersed into the community, albeit for only about an hour, but it told me much more of what really goes on in the community than I had learnt from three years of working in it. Different people came in to buy things, others for a chat and through the translation of the granddaughter I gained a much better 'feel' for the community. It is an experience that I shall never forget.

Guided participation

Rogoff (2003) believes that children are active participants in their culture and that in many circumstances adults, older siblings or elders in the community act as 'guided participants' to young children who are sometimes viewed by them as apprentices. Rogoff views this concept as existing not only within organised education but also that it is a very natural occurrence in communities. This suggests that participation in activities goes beyond being 'instructional' (p. 284) and about education, but also that it relates to skills and practices within communities. In the West with socioeconomic changes such as families living further away from each other and parents both needing to work, this concept has decreased slightly over the years. However, within communities where extended families live closely, guided participation is observed. Jessel *et al.* (2007) observed Bangladeshi communities living in the UK, where grandparents were involved with a food-growing project and encouraging their grandchildren to engage with maths- and science-related activities through gardening. The grandparents were observed to be passing on 'cultural knowledge' (p. 132) to their grandchildren and teaching them skills that could benefit other members of the community. While the grandparents were very active in the research, other skills were also observed and they were seen to be caring for the young children in other ways, such as by reading and telling stories as well as singing community songs in their home language, and the sharing of spiritual activities. These are all good demonstrations of how 'guided participation' can help children learn in a very informal and fun way. Maggi *et al.* (2005, p. 10) confirms this view by stating that 'families are the first environments with which children interact from birth. They are critically important in providing children with stimulation, support and nurturance.'

A concept also recognised by the EYFS (DCSF 2008) is that parents are a child's first educator. However, this can be seen as limited as it makes no mention of the role of grandparents or other community members who may also be involved in childcare.

It is also significant to note that siblings also are often involved in 'guided participation' activities, particularly in cultures where education is not compulsory. In some areas of Africa and India it is customary for boys to go to school and for girls to stay at home and help out with home-making and caring activities. Through this, they are encouraged to care for their younger siblings as well as learning cooking, sewing and other activities related to the home. While we in the West may see this as unusual, this custom occurs in many areas of the world. It is important that this is recognised in order that families coming from other cultures with different experiences of education can be welcomed and their customs understood.

Case study 3.2

Jon and Annu and their two children – Nasreen their daughter aged 5 and Soli their son aged 7 – had moved from India to the UK in order to find work and a better education for their children. Before coming to the UK they had been living near to their extended family in Delhi. The only school nearby was a boys' school that Soli attended, but the couple wanted their daughter, Nasreen, to be educated too.

Soli was a very bright child who enjoyed his studies. He particularly enjoyed learning to read and write and seemed to have a natural flare for mathematics, which he was encouraged to develop in school by his teachers and at home by his parents and grandparents.

The family settled in a city in the north of the UK where the children's father worked in the engineering department of the local university. The child's mother was a nurse in India but was unable to gain work in the UK until she had done further training into medical procedures used in the UK.

The children were attending a Church of England school in the UK and, although the family were Hindu, they liked the ethos of the school and were happy for their children to attend. However, after a couple of weeks in the school Soli started complaining that he was bored. Both John and Annu went in to speak to the teachers about this and discovered that unlike in Delhi, children in the UK did not receive such formal teaching as Soli had in India, and that the work that children in the UK were doing Soli had already done in his school in India the year before.

When they explained this dilemma to the teacher she suggested that they all work together to try and help Soli at school and to also give him homework that was more suited to his academic needs. They set out a programme for his learning and Soli stopped being bored and started to enjoy his education more.

> ### Reflection points
>
> - What would you do if a parent met with you and told you that their child was not enjoying their education?
>
> - How might you try to meet the individual needs of the child while also supporting their family?

Cultural tools

Many theorists including Bruner and Rogoff discuss how cultural tools can help and encourage children to learn. Smidt (2006) identifies cultural tools as being 'artefacts, symbols and systems developed in communities that are used to make, share and transform meanings' (p. 78). In the West these might be seen as pens, pencils, nursery rhymes, fairy stories, folklore, music and art. However, for children in other parts of the world these may differ. A child growing up in rural Africa, for example, may be more used to using twigs rather than pens and pencils, instead of having access to sand or cornflour they might use the soil under their feet. They may be more used to mixing mud and water to paint with and their artwork may be very different than that of children in the UK.

When I was in Ghana, the visiting members of the UK university set out to urge practitioners to encourage children in their settings to play. It was decided to create an activity whereby practitioners used what we thought were cultural tools that were found easily in the environment. We gave them foil, newspapers, pens, twigs, stones, cotton and water bottles. Using these props we encouraged the practitioners to retell a well-known story making items to illustrate the story through these 'tools'. Practitioners were given half an hour to create the props and they then had to retell the story to the group. To my surprise almost all of the groups retold Bible stories. I felt sure that if practitioners in the UK were asked to do this, stories such as *Elmer, The Gingerbread Man* or *We're All Going On a Bear Hunt* would have been adapted. This made me realise that in this particular culture faith was seen as a cultural tool as well. This goes along with the view of Smidt (2006) who recognises that children have to become knowledgeable about the cultural tools relevant to them, and suggests that these might be religious practices or belief systems.

Reflection points

- How do you view the role of faith/religion in a child's life?

- If you work with a child whose family follows a particular faith do you try to find out about it so that you are better informed?

- How would you encourage children in their journey of faith?

Liz Brooker

Liz Brooker is a reader at the Institute of Education in the UK and worked as a teacher before becoming a lecturer. Brooker is an expert in carrying out ethnographic research. 'Ethnography' is a term that is associated with research carried out by studying a group of people within their natural environment. It exemplifies Rogoff's view that to understand a culture one needs to become completely immersed in it. She carried out a large piece of research with communities in London particularly relating to their experience of children entering school for the first time. Part of this community was a large group of Bangladeshi families. Brooker was aiming to discover many aspects of family life as well as how families built relationships with the school, the views of parents in terms of their children's education and what impact the parents' education had on their children's learning.

Cultural context of play

One of the challenges that Brooker discovered was that of the different views of parents in relation to how children learn. Perhaps understandably, all parents wanted their children to be happy and to be able to learn enough to get a job and bring money home to their families. As suggested in the previous chapter, many parents did not engage with the concept that children learnt through play, instead they wanted children to learn to read and write because they viewed 'no benefit in playing' (Brooker 2002, p. 118) all day. They believed that children's academic development was being restricted by the focus on play and what they saw as the constant acceptance in the West that play is a medium to learning. This in itself also caused difficulties for bilingual workers in the school who felt torn between the traditions of the school and their need to support parents who could not understand the principle.

Like Rogoff, Brooker (2011) emphasises the need for practitioners to consider the cultural context of play in order to fully understand differences in how children learn and to try and seek a deeper understanding of the cultural beliefs that communities have around play. Brooker feels that not enough work has been done in the UK to fully understand differences in the way that children grow up and experience childhood. While she accepts that in the West play is seen as a vital component of learning, she also believes that there is a need to respect others' views of play and the 'cultural beliefs about the nature of children's learning' (p. 143). While carrying out research in Canada, Brooker (2011) heard differences in the views of young children. English children believed they came to school 'to play' whereas Bangladeshi children felt they came to school 'to learn'.

As with Bruner and Rogoff, Brooker (2002, p. 55) values those 'cultural artefacts and practices of communities' that 'run invisibly through family life' and are central to families' beliefs of how they want their children to grow and learn and that affect their well-being. She believes, as do I, that the aspirations of all families are that they want their children to be happy and do well in life. This may be because their parents were raised differently and did not aspire to as much as they would have liked or because they have high expectations of what their children can learn and become. This, I would suggest, is the same for families across the globe. However, Brooker (2002) suggests that when researchers look at the cultural element of how children grow up they can never fully put aside their own cultural perspectives on childhood. Brooker (2002) suggests that researchers need to take families' cultures and traditions more seriously and inquire more carefully into ways of learning that are carried out in the home.

The role of the environment in children's learning

Brooker, like Rogoff, recognises the role of the environment in shaping the culture of the child and suggests that for some this culture may be more about play and for others it may be more associated with doing things in the home that some may identify as being more aligned with 'work'. As Rogoff (2003, p. 282) suggests, for some families the 'learning process is the transformation of participation in cultural activities, by way of guided participation supported by peers and adults'.

From this we recognise that Brooker values the home experiences that children are involved with and views these as having the same importance as the education that children learn in settings. However, she poses the challenge that environments created by practitioners are potentially more akin to the 'Western' world and less to those of children from different cultures. How many settings have an array of dolls from other cultures? How many settings have dressing-up clothes from other cultures or a variety of large pieces of cloth from other countries that children can make into their own chosen outfits? Do children ever have the experience of soil and twigs being used in the setting rather than pens and paper? From my own experience of visiting settings in my role as a lecturer, I rarely see much evidence of cultural tools from other cultures. All of these activities would help participants to learn that children are not all the same and do not do the same things across the world.

Triangle of care

The term 'triangle of care' is a concept that Brooker has recently introduced into early years settings in the UK. It has been a concept used in health for many years to demonstrate the need for the patient, health care practitioner and the patient's carer to work more collegiately (Carers Trust 2013). At the turn of the century, with the ever-needed rise in childcare places across settings in the UK, the Birth to Three (Sure Start 2005) and Early Years Foundation Stage (DCSF 2008) curriculum recognised that young children should be given key workers who care for the child's needs during time spent in the setting. The key worker should also build a relationship with parents in order that the transition first from home to setting and then during different age phases can go as smoothly as possible. The key worker system is aligned to the view of Bowlby and Ainsworth that children, once they have formed an attachment to their parents, are then able to form an attachment with a 'significant other' when they are away from their parents (Henniger 2014). Brooker recognised that these relationships are not always easy to forge, especially if the key worker does not understand the culture from which the family is from or the parents have different views of the education system. However, it was her view that the lack of these strong respectful relationships can lead to the child feeling unwelcome in the setting.

Brooker (2016) believes that the 'triangle of care' is a respectful, reciprocal relationship between the key worker and child's main carer, which can 'provide a supportive environment for young children's development and wellbeing' (p. 71). The points of the triangle are labelled parent, child and carer and it is designed so that no relationship is hierarchical and thus all are equal parties in the relationship. The partnership needs to be open, trusting, responsive and respectful where the parents and key worker want to create the best provision for the child. It should also seek to discover as much about the child as possible – their likes and dislikes, routines, abilities, as well as the family background that the child has been brought up in. While there is acceptance through Brooker's writing (2010) that some parents may struggle with this kind of relationship, it is my view that practitioners should try as hard as they can to forge these strong relationships with carers so that they can fully understand the needs of all involved (see Figure 3.2).

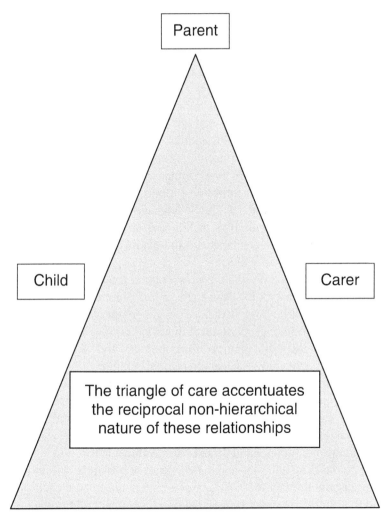

Figure 3.2 The triangle of care
Source: Brooker 2011.

Similarities and differences between the theorists

In looking at the works of Bruner, Bronfenbrenner, Rogoff and Brooker we can see many similarities. They all value the role of the adult and practitioner as being important in a child's life and position the child as being the central component of the relationship between them. They value the culture of the family and child, seeing it as a vital tenet in their lives. All discuss the fact that relationships between family, child and practitioner need to be born out of respect and a willingness to see difference and diversity as important.

Some of the differences emerge out of the way that different theorists view teachers. Bruner views adults as being an important part of a child's life in terms of their holistic development while acknowledging that they are essential in the way that children learn language. He uses the term 'language acquisition support system' to illustrate how practitioners can support children's language development. The role of bilingual staff particularly is highlighted, to support children who are learning more than one language and whose family language is not used predominantly in settings.

Bruner and Rogoff discuss the term 'cultural tools', which are items that are helpful to a child's learning and that differ depending on the culture that a child is brought up in. These are particularly important to acknowledge in settings, particularly if it is culturally diverse.

Rogoff suggests that grandparents, parents and siblings play a particular role in terms of teaching young children, in a way that is acknowledged in the West but perhaps not as formally as Rogoff does. She particularly discusses the role of grandparents and the way that they can help to teach children in ways that are natural, fun and informative.

Both Bronfenbrenner and Brooker discuss the relationships between all elements of a child's life and the way that each relate to one another. They discuss the fact that all parts of a child's life impact each other and that these can never be separated – this raises the importance of settings to forge strong relationships with carers in order to meet the needs of the child.

Conclusion

This chapter has focused on various theories around cultural diversity. The views of Jerome Bruner, Urie Bronfenbrenner, Barbara Rogoff and Liz Brooker have been considered and examined to seek out both similarities and differences. The chapter has also identified concepts in early years teaching that particularly relate to cultural diversity and the way that practitioners in the UK might work.

Chapter 4 will now discuss how children start to form ideas relating to who they are and where they come from, and the importance of cultural diversity to a child's burgeoning identity.

Points to consider

- Which of these theories can you best relate to in terms of working with families from other cultures? Why does it speak to you so clearly?

- What more do you need to do in your setting in order to support all parents?

- How do you view the role of the 'triangle of care'? Do you place importance on the need to build strong relationships with parents in your care?

Further reading

Brooker, L. (2002) *Starting School: Young Children Learning Cultures.* London: University of London.

Jessel, J., Gregory, E., Arju, T. and Ruby, M. (2004) Children and their grandparents at home: A mutually supportive context for learning and linguistic development. *English Quarterly* 36(4): 16–23.

References

Barr, K. and Borkett, P. (2015) Play with children from diverse cultures. In Moyes, J. (ed.) *The Excellence of Play* (pp. 275–285). Berkshire: Open University Press.

Boyatzis, Chris, J. (1998) A collaborative assignment on the role of culture in child development and education. *Teaching of Psychology* 25(3): 195–198.

Brooker, L. (2002) *Starting School: Young Children Learning Cultures*. London: University of London.

Brooker, L. (2010) Constructing the triangle of care: Power and professionalism in parent/practitioner relationships. *British Journal of Educational Studies* 58(2): 181–196.

Brooker, L. (2011) Taking children seriously: An alternative agenda for research? *Journal of Early Childhood Research* 9(2): 137–149.

Brooker, L. (2016) Childminders, parents and policy: Testing the triangle of care. *Journal of Early Childhood Research* 14(1): 69–83.

Brown, G. (1975) *Child Development*. Shepton Mallet: Open Books.

Bruner, J. (1996) *The Culture of Education*. Cambridge, MA: Harvard University Press.

Carers Trust (2013) *The Triangle of Care Carers Included: A Guide to Best Practice in Mental Health Care in England*. London: Carers Trust.

Department for Children, Schools and Families (DCSF) (2008) *Early Years Foundation Stage*. Nottingham: DCSF.

Government UK (2015) The Childcare Bill. www.gov.uk/governmentnews/governors.

Gray, C. and Macblain, S. (2015) *Learning Theories in Childhood* (2nd edition). London: Sage.

Henniger, M.L. (2014) *Teaching Young Children*. London: Pearson.

Jessel, J., Gregory, E., Arju, T. and Ruby, M. (2004) Children and their grandparents at home: A mutually supportive context for learning and linguistic development. *English Quarterly* 36(4): 16–23.

Kenner, C., Ruby, M., Gregory, E., Jessel, J. and Arju, T. (2007) Intergenerational learning between children and grandparents in East London. *Journal of Early Childhood Research* 5(3): 219–243.

Maggi, S., Irwin, A., Siddiqi, E. and Hertzman, C. (2005) Knowledge network for early child development: Analytic and strategic review paper: International perspectives on early child development. www.who.int/social_determinants/resources/ecd.pdf.

Nganga, L. (2009) Early childhood education programs in Kenya: Challenges and solutions. *Early Years: An International Journal of Research and Development* 29(3): 227–236.

Piaget, J. (1959) *The Language and Thought of the Child*. London: Routledge and Kegan Paul.

Rogoff, B. (2003) *The Cultural Nature of Human Development*. Oxford: Oxford University Press.

Smidt, S. (2006) *The Developing Child in the 21st Century: A Global Perspective on Child Development*. Oxon: Routledge.

Sure Start (2004) *Sure Start: For Everyone – Promoting Inclusion, Embracing Diversity, Challenging Inequality*. Nottingham: Sure Start.

Sure Start (2005) *Birth to Three Matters*. Nottingham: Sure Start.

Tobin, J., Hsueh, Y. and Karasawa, M. (2009) *Preschool in Three Cultures Revisited: China, Japan and the United States*. London: University of Chicago Press.

Waldren, J. and Kaminski, I. (2012). *Learning from the Children: Childhood, Culture and Identity in a Changing World*. Oxford: Berghahn Books.

Who are we?

The impact of cultural
diversity on a child's identity

Introduction

This chapter focuses on the important aspect of how a child develops
their identity. Brooker (2008) extols the fundamental importance of this
to young children, and yet it seems to be something that early years
practitioners find hard to interpret. Perhaps because they do not want
to offend families by asking questions about the many cultures that are
represented in the UK (Napier and Majhanovich 2013). However, it
is important that children grow up with a positive sense of who they
are, where they come from and where they are growing up. The early
years setting should be a positive place where children should be able
to play, explore and learn positively about diversity and difference in
order that they may grow up to be citizens of a world that is exciting
and diverse (Early Education 2012).

The notion of 'what is a child?' will be considered and childhood
will be discussed from both the perspective of a child growing up in
the UK and a child growing up in another area of the world. The chapter seeks to examine some of the challenges that families go through
when coming to the UK as asylum seekers and refugees and how
these families' views of education might differ from what is provided
in the UK. It will go on to discuss the meaning of identity and how
children start to recognise their own individuality when young before
deliberating on the meaning of words such as 'culture', 'religion' and
'spirituality' and how all of these can have an impact on a child's
growing sense of identity.

The last section focuses on negative aspects of life and how these may impact on families and their children. Finally, the chapter poses a challenge to practitioners to reflect on their own identity and to consider the importance of this to them and the children that they work with.

What is a child in the UK?

Over the years, there have been many different views regarding the role of the child in society. It was only around 200 years ago in the UK that children would be found working in mills and factories. The introduction of the Factory Act in 1819 (Herefordshire Council n.d.) restricted this to children over the age of 9 and it was decreed that children could only work in these conditions for 12 hours a day. In 1842, the Mines Act was introduced, which dictated that children under the age of 10 were prohibited from working anywhere in the mines, and that boys under 15 were not allowed to use machinery. In 1878 the Factory and Workshop Act banned children from working and the introduction of the Education Act in 1880 made it compulsory for all children aged between 5 and 10 to go to school. Thankfully, since then in the UK the Education Act passed in 1944 ensured that all children had access to education from the age of 4 to 16 (Gillard 2011). But what of children who are living in the developing world?

Is the concept of a child different in the developing world?

Earlier in this book (Chapter 1), we considered that only 18 per cent of children live in the developed world, thus leaving a further 82 per cent to grow up in very different situations. Children across the developing world are not as privileged as children growing up in the UK, as they do not have access to the range of services available here. In places like India, Bangladesh, Africa and Somalia, children still spend much of their time working and bringing essential money into families. In some of these areas, children are able to access education at various times in the day through charities providing educational support (Save the Children 2016). However, there seem to be far worse situations for children internationally. Child trafficking goes on in countries such as India, Guatemala and Indonesia. In these countries children may be taken from their homes and set to work as slaves for the rich and powerful (International Labour Organization 2016). Children affected by this may be taken to different countries and involved in illegal work in appalling conditions.

Otaigbe (2016) discusses how, in Nigerian society, views on the place of the child in a family differ enormously to those in the West. He speaks of an interview carried out with David Oyelowo, a Nigerian actor who was about to take up the role of Martin Luther King in the film *Selma*. David described his childhood as not just about the family bringing him up but 'wider Nigerian society raising him with a positive self-esteem that he thought of himself as a King, even in the humblest of circumstances' (p. 39).

This positive upbringing gave him the confidence and self-esteem that he would later need in life when acting. There is a proverb used in Africa, which states that 'It takes a village to raise a child' (Afriprov 1998). In Africa bringing up a child does not just relate to the family and extended family but becomes the responsibility of all adults living in the community.

In other areas of the world, as I have previously commented (Chapter 3), it is seen as being more important that boys receive education. A view that was highlighted when I was travelling in Africa recently and that will be discussed through the following reflective case study.

Case study 4.1

I visited an orphanage where many children lived, in what I viewed to be squalor. The majority of these children had been found wandering around villages, many of them young girls with special needs. Lamptey *et al.* (2015) discuss how in developing countries 'children with disabilities are often killed, chained, and isolated in rooms, hidden from public view by their families, or kept in institutions secluded from mainstream society' (p. 2).

A Ghanan charity had contacted the orphanage and wanted to pay for a number of children to attend the local school. The children that were chosen were all boys, thus confirming the view that it is more important for boys to be educated over girls and children who have special needs.

I found this situation to be abhorrent. The view that it is more important for boys to be educated is, I believe, a question of rights, which the UN Convention on the Rights of the Child (Unicef 1990) Article 28 upholds by suggesting that all children have a right to education and that it is the responsibility of adults to provide that education. This is another of those situations where we see differences in cultural beliefs, as in parts of the developing world it will be assumed that men will go out to work to bring in much-needed cash and to try and help families to get out of poverty, whereas girls are encouraged to help raise children and care for the home and wider family.

Reflection

- How do you feel that in some countries the most needy children in society have to live in these conditions?

- What could practitioners do in these cultures to ensure that all children receive an education tailored to their specific needs?

- Do you think it is right that practitioners and students from the UK should share their practice with practitioners?

In some areas of the world where communities still believe in witchcraft, children with special needs can be seen to be 'possessed by an evil spirit which will force them to cause harm to other family and community members' (Secker 2012, p. 23).

While practitioners may see this as an issue for the developing world only, it does relate to families who may have left their countries of origin and fled to the UK. I remember visiting a family once who originated from Africa and who suggested that their daughter who had special needs may have been 'born of the devil'. It took a great deal of time for the family to understand the fact that this was not the case and for them to accept this child as their daughter who, despite her special needs, needed support, encouragement and love from her family.

The dilemmas that refugees and asylum seekers experience when coming to the UK

So how might situations such as this have an impact on early years education in the UK? First, I would suggest that it is a social justice issue that practitioners in the UK need to know and be concerned about. In some areas of the UK cities are centres for families seeking asylum and may be known as Cities of Sanctuary. These are areas of the country that are 'committed to build a culture of hospitality and welcome especially for refugees seeking sanctuary from war and persecution' (City of Sanctuary 2016).

Statistics indicate that only 1 per cent of all families seeking asylum come to the UK (Refugee Council 2016). This means that they might have fled their countries of origin because it was no longer safe for them to be there, hoping to find a better life. Often, according to the UN Refugee Agency (n.d.), families live temporarily in many countries before coming to the UK to settle. A 40-year-old father makes this comment about coming to the UK to seek asylum: 'We had no choice other than to leave because it was not safe for our children, we left everything – our clothes, our furniture, even our food.'

Often, as the Local Government Association (2016) states, authorities place families in accommodation near to other family members. They ensure that families are in a home that is big enough for them, that they have access to medical centres, schools and good transport links. They also ensure that families can make links to places of worship that they may want to be involved with and supported by.

Families in this situation may be coming to educational provision in the UK finding a very different system than the one they left behind, if indeed their children received education in their country of origin. This means that practitioners need to be ready to support families and to explain why things in the UK are done as they are, while also understanding that an open and sensitive dialogue needs to be conducted. It is vital that families moving countries are well supported by staff who understand their situation and can offer help and advice. How children are affected by this transition can have an enormous effect on their identity and their sense of who they really are (Beckett et al. 2008).

Case study 4.2

Chol is a lady from Ethiopia who has come to live in the UK with her three children; two girls aged 5 and 7 and a little boy of around 9 months of age. Chol speaks very little English but appears to be a positive lady who tries to do the best for her family.

Chol attends a local church and has been assigned a translator who makes regular links with both the family and people within the church. This ensures that the congregation are able to support her with belongings and furniture and to try and communicate with her on Sundays.

The children both attend a local primary school, which is in a very multicultural community. Here the girls are supported in all areas of education and the bilingual support workers try to support Chol. However, education in the UK is very different to that in Ethiopia and the girls are both finding it all very strange. They enjoy playtimes because they can play together but they find the time in lessons quite lonely. While the school do employ bilingual support workers, they are in the main from Pakistan or Eastern European countries, so struggle to communicate with the family.

What is identity?

The term 'identity' is a concept that is organic. It evolves throughout life as children develop, learn and ask questions relating to their lives. Gunaratnam (2003) suggests that identity is 'a process through which multiple and changing subject positions are given a sense of coherence' (p. 11).

The United Nations Convention on the Rights of the Child (UNCRC) (Unicef 1990) recognises the need for children to have an identity through Article 8, which points out that 'every child has the right to an identity'. This ensures that children have a legal identity, which in the UK is brought about by the registration of a child within six weeks of birth.

Brooker (2008, p. 4) views identity as 'multidimensional' with characteristics such as the child's name and nationality established and registered at birth. Children then go on to develop other more personal identities through their life course. Aistear (n.d.) suggest that a child's identity first relates to their place within the family, their parents' roles in the community and their culture. They go on to suggest that identity also reflects the child's characteristics, likes and dislikes, self-esteem and personality.

Barley (2014) makes a similar suggestion that some parts of our identity are anchored. These might relate to our position in the family, culture, faith, nationality and gender. However, *The Observer* reported in 2016 that higher levels of children under the age of 10 want to change their gender at some time in their lives. It can be argued that this suggests gender can no longer be seen as a static part of identity. Barley also asserts the view that areas of identity may change as children grow while suggesting that at times it is hard to 'delineate' (p. 52) aspects of one's identity.

Issa and Hatt (2013) state that the culture children are born into is a large aspect of their identity. They go on to suggest that the two terms, 'identity' and 'culture' are interchangeable and cannot be separated. They discuss the view that cultural diversity relates to 'a dynamic process which facilitates the transformation of particular social and cultural characteristics of the child's home and community' (p. 6).

Rogoff (2003) suggests that there can be a tendency to use a single category to group people's identities, as you might be expected to do if you were asked to complete a questionnaire. So this may be in terms such as ethnicity, race or socioeconomic grouping. Rogoff (2003) goes on to imply that these 'boxes' are unhelpful and encourage the categorisation or homogenisation of certain groups based around 'race, ethnicity and socioeconomic class' (p. 77). She espouses that culture should never be recognised as a 'sole agent' of a child's identity as it is just one factor of it. Barley (2014) also indicates that a child's religious identity can also be a 'dominant status' (p. 76) depending on how much their family are involved in religious practice. It is important to focus on how it is that a child starts to form ideas about their identity.

How does a child start to recognise their identity?

Self-concept

Before the age of 2, a child is very much 'at one' with their parents or main carers and they start to slowly develop a sense of self-concept – that is who they are. They feel safe when they are with their family and see themselves very much as part of their parents' lives. During this time, babies are forging those important links of attachment (O'Donovan and Melnyczuk 2015) with their main carers and are beginning to find out who they are, what place they have within their family and who is important to them. They are learning that communication is reciprocal and reliant on someone else noticing them and communicating with them. They are, as Aistear commented (n.d.), getting to know their community and their role within this. Bronfenbrenner (1979) maintains that the microsystem of the child and immediate family starts to relate to the mesosystem, which includes the community in which the family live. For some this may mean that they are learning about what is known as their nuclear family, with whom they live. For others, growing up in wider family groupings means they may be learning from their 'guided participants' (Rogoff 2003) who may be grandparents, aunts, uncles and cousins or community elders.

The emergence of a child's sense of identity

However, at around the age of 2 things start to change. Children start to acknowledge that they are a person in their own right. This can be especially recognised through their language skills. Prior to the age of 2, Simpson (2011) suggests that children use the term 'my' or their name as a prefix to an action they are taking, however, once they turn 2 years old they are more likely to use the term 'I', thus recognising that they have an opinion and a place in society. At this time in a child's life we sometimes observe a rise in temper tantrums. This is not because the child is trying to be malicious or cause their parents extra stress but because their world has suddenly changed, they are aware that their communication skills matter, and they are testing out boundaries to see how far they can go (O'Donovan and Melnyczuk 2015).

However, these situations that children experience before the age of 2 do have an effect on their burgeoning sense of identity. Children will have an awareness of the language used at home (Issa and Hatt 2013) and how this may be different in certain circumstances or with different people. They may also be hearing and 'playing with' more than one language in order that they become bilingual in the future. Dunn (2004) accentuates the view that non-verbal communication, conversations and engagement between children and their elders, as well as the use of electronic media, all play a part in helping a child to find out about their own identity. Through these interactions, and also increasingly today from electronic technology, children are continually learning about the world around them, where they have come from, who they belong to, how their peers and adults listen to them and give them positive attention. This sense of identity continues to grow throughout their lives and as shown above, a child's culture is a vital part of that identity.

Reflection points

- If someone asked you to identify who you were, what answer would you give?

- Think about your identity – how has it changed throughout your life?

- Do you ever consider how children define themselves?

- What more could you do as a practitioner to support children to gain a positive self-image and to develop their self-esteem?

What is culture?

'Culture' is a word that, like 'identity', is often hard to define and seems to mean different things to different people. It is often a word that gets confused with issues relating to faith. People become mystified as to whether certain aspects or habits of someone's life relates to culture or faith. Baldock (2010) defines culture as being about the traditions and customs that bind groups of people together. Smidt (2006) views this as a superficial explanation that suggests that culture is fixed and unchangeable and does not accept that artefacts, values, music, food and clothes are an important aspect of culture. Vianna and Stetsenko (2006) view the term as being a 'living continuous flow of practices which are enacted by different generations of people' (p. 90). This view values culture as being similar to identity – it is changeable, dynamic and evolves over time. Korbin (2002, p. 638) endorses this view while also suggesting that different communities are always 'adapting to changing circumstances', therefore stressing the view that cultures reflect historical and familial changes. A view shared by McMullen (2017) who values the many different 'constructs' and understandings of cultures, which he suggests can never be fully understood 'from the outside' (p. 9).

When one considers the mixed messages that children get about culture, it often relates to aspects of the traditions and festivals that are celebrated around the UK. A child coming to the 'Westernised' world at Christmas might think that this celebration is about Santa Claus, snow and reindeers (Borkett 2012). This is a cultural view and is not the Christian view of Christmas, which is about God taking on the form of a baby to come to the world. Likewise when celebrating Easter, children hear about chickens, bunnies and chocolate – cultural ideas of Easter and not the Christian story of Christ's death and the message of the new life that people can come to know through Him. The same could be said for Hindus who celebrate Diwali. Again, as with Christmas, settings celebrate this because it is about light and the celebration of light coming at the end of dark – children often make little Diwali lights but there is much more to this celebration than lights, as the festival is celebrated to signify good over evil (Reference.com n.d.). Similarly when settings recognise Ramadan and celebrate Eid they may not mention that it is a thanksgiving to the God Allah for all the blessings that he gives to Muslims (Maqsood 2009). Not taking note of the 'wholeness' of celebrations and customs, which might also include the Jewish faith and Sikhism, may appear to be tokenistic – an issue that will be discussed later in the chapter. Barley (2014) asserts the view that for children of faith it is vital that their religion is acknowledged and celebrated in settings.

Reflection points

- How would you define your culture?

- Is it possible for you to define yourself according to your culture?

- How good is your setting at encouraging children to think about differences in the ways that people and communities live?

What is religion?

As with 'identity' and 'culture', it is important to consider that this is another term with many different meanings. There will be meanings derived from different sources, e.g. sociologists will view religion differently from proponents of specific religions. Myers (1997) views religion as being a dynamic relationship with someone who is 'central and has value and power in life' (p. 68). For a Christian this would be God, for Muslims Allah. Hindus worship many Gods but also think of Brahman as their main god. Sikhs view Ik Onkar as a 'representation of the united God in Sikhism' (Stone 2008). The Joseph Rowntree Trust (2008) suggests that rather than just being 'a set of behaviours linked to a higher being', religion and faith have the power to 'profoundly influence many people's lives' (p. 1). Mahoney (2010, p. 221) asserts that 'religion is distinctive because it incorporates peoples' perceptions of the "sacred" into the search for significant goals and values'.

Bartkowski, Xu and Levin (2008) and Kohut (1985) view religious involvement as a cultural resource that can help to bind families particularly during times of discord and argument. However, Mahoney (2010) argues that religion can also lead to conflict in families, especially when parents do not share the same religion. Rather than being something that joins groups of people together under a common name, many people see religion as something divisive and that has the capacity to separate people with dividing views as to whether or not these higher powers that all religions speak of, truly exist (Ashton 2000). However, whatever one's own beliefs are, there needs to be an acceptance in early years settings of the significance of religion for many. Families coming to the UK from overseas often have a strong faith and their children are encouraged to develop their faith too. Many of these have difficulty relating to a country that seems a little afraid to speak of faith-based issues in case they offend (Bartkowski *et al.* 2008).

The Early Years Foundation Stage (EYFS) (DFE 2012) emphasises the view that children should be taught about the similarities and differences of each other's lives. However, it does not suggest which religious festivals should be celebrated and it says nothing particular about the role of religion in a child's life. So how might a child demonstrate that they have an awareness of a higher being in their lives?

What is spirituality?

Bone (2008) suggests that 'spirituality' is another term that means different things to different people. Some view it as being related to religion but others see it differently, believing it offers a 'connected-ness' (p. 344) to nature and the universe and an opportunity for people to appreciate the 'wonder and mystery in everyday life' (Ratcliff and Nye 2006).

The UN Convention on the Rights of the Child (Unicef 1990) states in Article 14.3 that all children should have the right to 'manifest' their faith or belief providing that this does not hinder other children following a different faith path. Article 30 continues to suggest that children should receive the opportunity, wherever they live, to profess practices that relate to their own faith or belief systems (Unicef 1990). This perhaps subscribes to the view that children have the potential to be 'spiritual beings' (Hardy 1996, p. 10).

More recently, Hay and Nye (2006) have viewed spirituality as being something that is 'biologically built' (p. 63), which may not nec-essarily pertain to any particular religion. Hyde (2004) follows this view while also extolling the view of Ranson (2002) that religion and spirituality are not disparate elements of humanity but are intercon-nected. Holmes (2002) continues in this vein suggesting that places of worship should foster children's beliefs. However, she has a word of warning for the educational system, which she believes can crush or sabotage children's burgeoning spirituality by not recognising it as an essential part of children's development.

As stated earlier, in terms of current early years education, the EYFS curriculum (DFE 2012) followed in all early childhood settings throughout England pays little attention to the issue of children's spir-ituality. It seeks to accept the fact that all children are unique and through that uniqueness may follow certain faith or beliefs alongside their parents. However, in other areas of the world spirituality is recognised as a vital tenet in a family's life and a child's development. In New Zealand the Te Whariki Early Childhood Curriculum (education.gov.nz n.d.) has four main themes: (1) empowerment, (2) holistic development, (3) family and community and (4) relationships. Within the holistic development strand the spiritual notion of a child is integral, and it is recognised as being an essential part of a child learning about who they are culturally, socially and individually. In the Te Whariki curriculum all four areas of a child's development are woven together. The programme is likened to a mat where these areas are equally woven together – all of them being essential to a child's development rather than being tagged on to particular festivals as is done in the UK. Bone (2008) warns that spirituality is often conceptualised as being 'somewhere on the periphery' (p. 347) of life and draws on Bruner's (1990) work, who views culture and religion as an essential part of a child's concept of themselves.

Figure 4.1 Spirituality

For me, awe and wonder is clearly being demonstrated by the picture shown in Figure 4.1. It is of a little girl at a wedding. A rose has come detached from her aunt's wedding bouquet and has dropped to the ground. While running with her cousin she finds the flower and then picks it up and sits looking at it – gently fingering the petals, smelling the scent for around five minutes. She doesn't need to speak – the concentration on her face is enough to tell me that she has found something precious. She gently gives it back to her aunt and then continues to play.

I would suggest, like Bone (2008), children are able to see and experience that connectedness to nature and to the world around them. The fact that they like to learn through exploration, stamp in mud, have a fascination with water and how it flows, love blowing bubbles and seeing the colours in them demonstrates to me the awe and wonder that children experience.

Reflection points

- What is your view on spirituality, do you see it as part of religion or an aspect of all people?

- Have you ever considered that children might be spiritual beings?

- What might you do in your setting to encourage children to be spiritual?

- Do you have areas in your setting where children can go to 'just be', to think about who they are, where they come from, the 'special people' in their lives?

Can anything hinder a child's growing identity?

Racism

It is imperative when relating to children's identity to be aware that if a child grows up with negativity in terms of their culture or any other area of their life that this can have a major effect on the way that the child views themselves and their identity. A view endorsed by Swadener (2008), who states that: 'Children who learn that their family, faith or cultural group is stigmatised, or otherwise discriminated against, need additional support for their growing self-esteem and self-worth' (p. 22).

It is vital therefore that when practitioners are working with children that they do not just experience 'Westernised' notions of childhood. They may be growing up in the UK but essentially all children need to experience the traditions, festivals and cultural aspects of the world that they live in. This can be done through storytelling, singing, drama, role-play and getting to know about the 'cultural tools' (Rogoff 2003) that come from their particular country of origin. As we read earlier, young children's identities are often multiple and complex and so they need practitioners to be interested in all areas of a child's life.

Here we see the importance of adults and practitioners who will respect children for who they are, will form strong reciprocal, respectful relations with them and who will help them to understand their lives and their growing sense of identity. Smidt (2006) suggests that children construct their identities partially from how they are represented in society and in places that they attend. She suggests that if a child is an only black child in a particularly white community, that they may feel lonely, ostracised and may be discriminated against.

Media

At this point in the chapter it is important to consider other aspects of a child's life that may have an impact on the way they identify themselves. The Canadian Paediatric Society (2003) indicates that while television can educate children about differences and diversity, it can also stereotype people and cultures (Johanssen 2012). It is suggested that images of children from different cultures, who have special needs or who live in families that may be different in some way are rarely represented on children's TV shows. Palmer (2006) discusses the view that children need positive role models who come from a range of cultures in their lives, whose characteristics and qualities they may try to emulate. As Chambers (2012) suggests, TV rarely portrays children as members of a society that is diverse and exciting. If they do, they paint a picture of families where parents are both black and both white – in the twenty-first century it is important to acknowledge that many families are made up of a mix of cultures yet these are rarely endorsed through the medium of TV.

When I was growing up in the late 1950s and early 1960s, a period of time when many people were coming into the UK from various different parts of the world, a song was often heard on the radio and TV that talked about race and people. Some of its lyrics were: 'What we need is a great big melting pot. Big enough to take the world and all it's got and keep it stirring for a hundred years or more and turn out coffee colored people by the score' (BlueMink 1969).

At the time the song was viewed as encouraging as it related to people who were black positively and suggested that when white and black come together they produce something new, which takes on features of both cultures. Vandenbroeck (2008) views this as 'colour blindness' that fails to accept differences in people, instead it prefers to 'treat all children as equal' (p. 28). Vandenbroeck goes on to suggest that this can happen when people welcome others from different cultures but expect them to assimilate into the dominant culture without recognising differences that are dynamic and diverse.

Yoon (2017) writes about her daughter's wish to buy a 'princess doll' who had the same colour skin as her. She was growing up in America with her black American mother and white father. Her parents were keen to ensure that that she grows up to value her race and colour and tell her that she is beautiful. However, trying to find a doll that was a princess and black was proving difficult. She goes on to challenge toy manufacturers, media and TV programmes to produce more dolls, books and programmes that positively represent people of colour. While Disney does produce black characters the Global Spectrum (2017) suggests that they do not fully represent ethnic diversity, arguing that 'evil characters are typically given darker coloring while heroes are often white in Disney films' (p. 1).

Parents

It is important to consider when discussing issues around race and identity that parents can often have an impact on a child's sense of identity. As I stated in 2012, children come from families who live in different communities and have different views around diversity and inclusion. Families often form their own views of society through their own previous experiences, transitions and views picked up through the media and, more importantly today, social media. The last chapter introduced the notion of Bronfenbrenner's ecological systems theory (Gray and Macblain 2015). He later added to the theory a fifth layer, which he referred to as the *chronosystem*. This final system relates to environmental issues and transitions that people make in life and the effect that these can have on parents initially and subsequently to their children.

In 2016 a TV programme followed a black mother and her children over a week and demonstrated the lengths she went to to ensure that her children did well at school and became active members of their communities. While being interviewed the mother was asked why it was that her children belonged to so many sports and community groups and after school activities – she responded that she was 'acutely aware that even as second generation immigrants her children would always be viewed as immigrants and that the opportunities for them would not be available unless they were at a certain standard of education' (BBC 2016).

Here we see an example of Bronfenbrenner's chronosystem, whereby the mother herself had struggled through education when she came to the UK, so she was doing all she could so that her children would not experience the lack of opportunities that she and her husband felt during that time.

Tokenism

The term 'tokenism' relates to viewing a child's culture or home life as static. Families' identities are reduced and thought to be the same as any other person who may be part of that cultural group. For instance, tokenism would say that every British person lives in exactly the same way, speaks the same language, wears the same kinds of clothes and eats the same kind of food. This is just not true but how often is it the way that different cultures are explained in educational settings? Seeing groups of people like this negates and can stigmatise particular groups. As Brooker (2008) stresses, it is vital that while children are wrestling with learning about themselves and who they are they need 'parents, professionals and other adults who become a major conduit through which children can be assured positive identities whilst recognising that children's own agency is also central' (p. 12).

As suggested by Connolly (2008), perhaps it is far too easy to pay lip service to cultural practices and festivals without really discovering the true sense and purpose of traditions that cultures hold dear.

Reflection

While writing this chapter I have been trying to develop a metaphor for what I see identity looking like and for me it is like a tree (see Figure 4.2). To begin with there are roots – these are those aspects of identity that cannot be changed. Where one is born, the family you are brought up by, the culture you grow up in and the traditions attached to this. Other aspects of life become the trunk of the tree – this might relate to particular characteristics, the physical aspects that might have been inherited from parents, people who might have influenced your views and opinions. The leaves represent aspects of your identity that may evolve, develop and change as you go through life and could relate to attributes and skills that may be developed. They could also relate to faith-based principles that may be part of life and ways that you choose to live in relation to these. Trees change colour and leaves blow away, which may illustrate the changing identities as people grow through life and illustrate the fact that parts of our identity are always evolving.

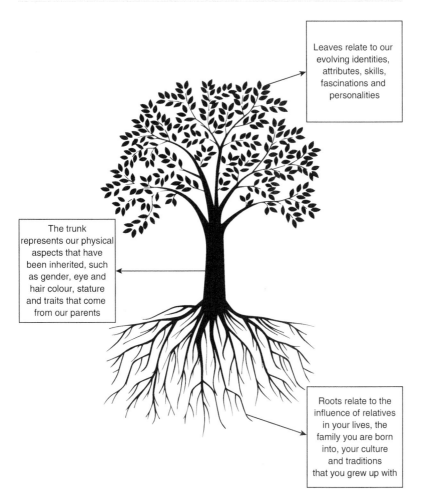

Leaves relate to our evolving identities, attributes, skills, fascinations and personalities

The trunk represents our physical aspects that have been inherited, such as gender, eye and hair colour, stature and traits that come from our parents

Roots relate to the influence of relatives in your lives, the family you are born into, your culture and traditions that you grew up with

Figure 4.2 The tree of life

Conclusion

This chapter has focused on the important aspect of how children develop their identity while discussing the differing views of the role of children from across the world. It has raised the importance of children acknowledging and recognising their own culture and faith as they grow up and the impact that these have on their developing sense of identity.

It has sought to discover the meaning of the word 'child' and how this differs across the world. While examining the plight of families and children coming to the UK as asylum seekers and refugees, it has also explored how different views of education might overwhelm and confuse families. The meaning of the term 'identity' has been introduced and has reflected on the way that children begin to form ideas relating to their identity. The terms 'culture', 'religion' and 'spirituality' have been examined and the importance all of these can have on a child's growing sense of identity discussed.

The last section of the chapter focused on some of the negative aspects of life and how these may impact on families and their children as well as the child's burgeoning identity. Finally, through practical application the chapter has challenged practitioners to reflect on their own identity and to consider the importance of this to them and the children that they work with.

The next chapter discusses how practitioners should work with parents and carers to ensure that all families are welcomed into early years settings.

Points to consider

- Think about your life and identity. Try to consider it to be like a tree.

- What are the foundations of your life that cannot be changed and are fixed?

- What elements of your life can be seen as the trunk of the tree and might relate to particular characteristics, the physical aspects that might have been inherited from parents, people who might have influenced your views and opinions?

Then consider what leaves may make up the remainder of the tree. These could be aspects of life that you are trying hard to change. Ethical aspects of your life that may relate to faith or the way that you choose to live your life.

Now consider this tree to be previous, it is you and illustrates important aspects of your life. Reflect on this and think about the way that you might encourage the children that you work with to become like trees – full of hope and promise, proud of all aspects of life that make them who they are.

Further reading

Bone, J. (2008) Creating relational spaces: Everyday spirituality in early childhood settings. *European Early Childhood Education Research Journal* 16(3): 265–276.

Brooker, L. (2008) Defining positive identity. In Woodhead, M. and Oates, J. (eds) *Developing Positive Identities: Diversity and Young Children. Early Childhood in Focus* (vol. 3, p. 10). Milton Keynes: The Open University.

Connolly, P. (2008) Positive identities may lead to negative beliefs in developing positive identities – diversity and young children. *Early Childhood in Focus* (vol. 3, p. 42). Milton Keynes: The Open University.

Yoon, N. (19 August 2017) We don't make princesses in those colours. www.theguardian.com.

References

African Proverb of the Month (1998) It takes a village to raise a child. www.afriprov.org/african-proverb-of-the-month/23-1998proverbs/137-november-1998-proverb.html.

Aistear (n.d.) Identity and belonging. www.ncca.biz/aistear/pdfs/principlesthemes.

Ashton, E. (2000) *Religious Education in the Early Years*. Padstow: T.J. International.

BBC (15 March 2016) Identity 2016: How are you changing? www.bbc.co.uk/news/world-35757586.

Baldock, P. (2010) *Understanding Cultural Diversity in the Early Years*. London: Sage.

Barley, R. (2014) *Identity and Social Interaction in a Multi-Ethnic Classroom*. London: Tufnell Press.

Bartkowski, J.P., Xu, X. and Levin, M.L. (2008) Religion and child development: Evidence from the Early Childhood Longitudinal Study. *Social Science Research* 37(1): 18–36.

Beckett, C., Hawkins, H., Rutter, M. and Sonuga-Barke, E. (2008) The importance of cultural identity in adoption: A study of young people adopted from Romania. *Journal of Adoption and Fostering* 32(3): 9–22.

Blue Mink (1969) Melting pot. www.songlyrics.com/blue-mink/melting-pot-lyrics.

Bone, J. (2008) Creating relational spaces: Everyday spirituality in early childhood settings. *European Early Childhood Education Research Journal* 16(3): 265–276.

Borkett, P. (2012) Diversity and inclusion in the early years. In Kay, J. (ed.) *Good Practice in the Early Years* (pp. 91–115). London: Continuum.

Bronfenbrenner, U. (1979) *The Ecology of Human Development*. Cambridge, MA: Harvard University Press.

Brooker, L. (2008) Defining positive identity. In Woodhead, M. and Oates, J. (eds) *Developing Positive Identities: Diversity and Young Children. Early Childhood in Focus* (vol. 3, p. 10). Milton Keynes: The Open University.

Bruner, J.S. (1990) *Acts of Meaning*. Cambridge, MA: Harvard University Press.

Canadian Paediatric Society (2003) Impact of media use on children and youth. *Paediatric Child Health* 8(5): 301–306.

Chambers, D. (2012) *A Sociology of Family Life: Change and Diversity in Intimate Relations*. Cambridge: Polity Press.

City of Sanctuary (2016) https://cityofsanctuary.org.

Connolly, P. (2008) Positive identities may lead to negative beliefs in developing positive identities – diversity and young children. *Early Childhood in Focus* (vol. 3, p. 42). Milton Keynes: The Open University.

Department for Education (DFE) (2012) *The Early Years Foundation Stage*. London: DFE.

Dunn, J. (2004) *Children's Friendships: The Beginnings of Intimacy*. Oxford: Blackwell.

Early Education (2012) *Development Matters in the Early Years Foundation Stage*. London: Early Education.

Education.gov.nz (n.d.) Te Whariki. www.education.govt.nz/early-childhood/teaching-and-learning/ece-curriculum/te-whariki/principles-strands-goals.

Gillard, D. (2011) Education in England: A brief history. www.educationeng land.org.uk/history/chapter05.html.

The Global Spectrum (2017) Intercultural perspectives and intercultural topics. www.theglobalspectrum.org/home/2017/2/21/disney.

Gray, C. and Macblain, S. (2015) *Learning Theories in Childhood* (2nd edition). London: Sage.

Gunaratnam, Y. (2003) *Researching Race and Ethnicity: Methods, Knowledge and Power*. London: Sage.

Hardy, A. (1966) *The Divine Flame: An Essay Towards a Natural History of Religion*. London: Collins.

Hay, D. and Nye, R. (2006) The spirit of the child. *Pastoral Care in Education* 24(3): 41–48.

Herefordshire Council (n.d.) UK child labour and education laws: A history. http://htt.herefordshire.gov.uk/herefordshires-past/the-post-medieval-period/agriculture-and-industry/child-labour.

Holmes, T. (2002) Children with time and space to explore spirituality. www.lexisnexis.com.lcprosy.shu.ac.uk/uk/legal/auth/bridge.do.

Hyde, B. (2004) Children's spirituality and the good shepherd experience. *The Official Journal of the Religious Education Association* 99(2): 137–150.

International Labour Organization (ILO) (2016) Trafficking in children. www.ilo.org/ipec/areas/Traffickingofchildren/lang--en/index.htm.

Issa, T. and Hatt, A. (2013) *Language, Culture and Identity in the Early Years*. London: Bloomsbury.

Johansen, E.J. (2012) The portrayal of family in advertising: Children's perspectives. *Dissertations and Theses from the College of Business Administration, Paper 34*. http://digitalcommons.unl.edu/businessdiss/34.

Joseph Rowntree Trust (2008) *The Influence of Religious Beliefs on Parenting, from the Perspectives of Both Adolescents and Parents*. York: Joseph Rowntree Trust.

Kohut, H. (1985) *Self-Psychology and the Humanities: Reflection on a New Psychoanalytical Approach*. New York: Norton & Co.

Korbin, J.E. (2002) Culture and child maltreatment: Cultural competence and beyond. *Journal of Child Abuse and Neglect* 26: 637–644.

Lamptey, D., Villeneuve, M., Minnes, P. and McColl, M.A. (2015) Republic of Ghana's policy on inclusive education and definitions of disability. *Journal of Intellectual Disabilities* 12: 108–111. doi:10.1111/jppi.12114.

Local Government Association (2016) *Syrian Refugee Resettlement: A Guide for Local Authorities*. London: Local Government Association.

Mahoney, A. (2010) Religion in families 1999–2009: A relational spirituality framework. *Journal of Marriage and Families* 72(4): 805–827.

McMullen, J. (2017) *The Baha'is of America: The Growth of a Religious Movement*. New York: New York University Press.

Maqsood R.W. (2009) *Teach Yourself Islam*. Oxon: Bookpoint.

Myers, B.K. (1997) *Young Children and Spirituality*. London: Routledge.

Napier, D.B. and Majhanovich, S. (2013) *Education, Dominance and Identity*. Istanbul: Sense.

O'Donovan, C. and Melnyczuk, V. (2015) Brain development and play. In Moyles, J. (ed.) *The Excellence of Play* (4th edition). Berkshire: Open University Press.

Otaigbe, O.O. (2016) *Building Cultural Intelligence in Church and Ministry*. Bloomington, IN: AuthorHouse.

Palmer, S. (2006) *Toxic Childhood: How the Modern World Is Damaging Our Children and What We Can Do about It*. London: Orion Books.

Ranson, D. (2002) *Across the Great Divide: Bridging Spirituality and Religion Today*. Strathfield, NSW: St Pauls.

Ratcliffe, D. and Nye, R. (2006) Childhood spirituality: Strengthening the research foundation. In Roehlkepartain, E.C., Ebstyne King, P., Wagener, L. and Benson, P.L. (eds) *The Handbook of Spiritual Development in Children in Childhood and Adolescence* (pp. 473–483). Thousand Oaks, CA: Sage.

Reference.com (n.d.) What are some important Hindu religious holidays? www.reference.com/holidays-celebrations/important-hindu-religious-holidays.

The Refugee Council (2016) Tell it like it is: The truth about refugees and asylum seekers – separating the fact from the fiction. www.refugeecouncil.org.uk/what_we_do/refugee_services.

Rogoff, B. (2003) *The Cultural Nature of Human Development*. New York: Oxford University Press.

Save the Children (2016) What we do? *Education*. www.savethechildren.org.uk/about-us/what-we-do/education.

Secker, E. (2012) Witchcraft stigmatization in Nigeria: Challenges and successes in the implementation of child rights. *International Journal of Social Work* 56(1): 22–36.

Simpson, K. (2011) The unfolding self: The essence of personality. In House, R. (ed.) *Too Much, Too Soon: Early Learning and the Erosion of Childhood* (pp. 147–159). Gloucestershire: Hawthorn Press.

Smidt, S. (2006) *The Developing Child in the 21st Century: A Global Perspective on Child Development*. London: Routledge.

Stone, J. (8 May 2008) What do Sikhs believe? *Religious beliefs of sikhism questioned in the wake of sunday's shooting*. www.ibtimes.com.

Swadener, B. (2008) Supporting identities through parenting programmes. In Woodhead, M. and Oates, J. (eds) *Developing Positive Identities: Diversity and Young Children: Early Childhood in Focus* (vol. 3, p. 22). Milton Keynes: The Open University.

Unicef (1990) UN Convention on the Rights of the Child. www.unicef.org.uk/what-we-do/un-convention-child-rights.

United Nations High Commission for Refugees (n.d.) Iraq emergency. www.unhcr.org/uk/iraq-emergency.html.

Vandenbroeck, B. (2008) The challenge for early childhood education and care. In Woodhead, M. and Oates, J. (eds) *Developing Positive Identities: Diversity and Young Children: Early Childhood in Focus* (vol. 3, p. 26). Milton Keynes: The Open University.

Vianna, E. and Stetsenko, A. (2006) Embracing history through transforming it. *Journal of Theory and Psychology* 16(1): 81–108.

Yoon, N. (19 August 2017) We don't make princesses in those colours. www.theguardian.com.

What should practitioners do?

5 Working with families

Introduction

This chapter will focus on the importance of working closely with parents/carers in a sensitive and non-judgemental way. The need to work with parents has been an important aspect of the Early Years Foundation Stage (EYFS) since its inception in 2008 (DCSF 2008) and since then while this requirement has remained it has changed slightly depending on which political party has been in power. It suggests that parents are a child's first and enduring educator and stresses the requirement for early years settings to work alongside parents as a partnership. However, that can be challenging for practitioners as no two families are the same and whatever the family's dominant culture, parents all bring with them different life histories, which may have an impact on how they parent their own children (Bruner 2000).

The chapter will discuss some of these differences and compare and contrast how families living in the developing world focus so much on education and why this is so important to them. It will also seek to differentiate terms such as 'immigrant', 'refugee' and 'asylum seeker' as it is paramount that practitioners understand why it is that people move from their home countries to seek asylum in the UK as well as the impact this might have on their understanding of the English education system. It will discuss areas of policies that particularly relate to families from other cultures such as the Equality Act (2010), the Early Years Foundation Stage (EYFS) (2017) and the Children and Families Act (2012). Consideration will finally be made of the way families have changed over the past 50 years and the importance of working particularly with families who are often labelled as being 'hard to reach' (Weinberger, Pickstone and Hannon 2005).

What is a family?

To attempt to answer this question may seem a little crazy as it is virtually impossible to 'pigeon hole' any particular family to be 'the norm' or an 'ideal'. Families are all different and have changed greatly over the past 50 years. In recent years there have been many studies carried out in order to attempt to define the role of the family, particularly in the West (Flandrin 1979; Shorter 1975; Stone 1977). However, all of these studies have looked particularly at families living in the Western world and not at families across the world. However, Chambers (2012) suggests that with the growth of globalisation and the ease of worldwide travel, geographical distances that were once difficult to maintain now enable families to travel across the world and live in different countries. Chambers (2012) goes on to suggest that recent changes to family structures and a growth in women's employment have had an impact on the role of families and the need for early childcare (ONS 2013).

However, with these changes there has also been a rise in women from developing countries coming to the West to work, particularly in the hospitality industry or working as au pairs for more wealthy Western families, and then sending money home to their families to help educate their children in their country of origin. At the other end of the spectrum, women from the developing world are sadly sometimes groomed and used as sex workers or traffickers in the Western world (Campbell-Barr, Georgeson and Selbie 2016).

Changes to family structure

Alongside the need for more women to go out to work there have been many other changes to the way the family has evolved in the Western world. The idea of the nuclear family as espoused by Parsons (1971) where a family is made up of mother, father and two children has changed greatly in the twenty-first century. Previously, fathers were expected to work to provide money for the family and mothers commonly stayed at home to care, primarily for the home and children. However, in the light of more feminist approaches to the family that started to emerge in the late 1970s, the idea of the father being the sole breadwinner started to change and more women chose to return to work after having their children. Feminists such as Greer (1970) applauded this move and it was around this time that, as reported in Chapter 3, there was an increase in the number of early years settings across the UK.

Another change brought about around this time was an increase in cohabitation, where rather than marrying, men and women choose to live together and have children before they marry. Lewis (2001) makes the suggestion that the 'moral distinction, between marriage and cohabitation is changing and suggests that young people no longer need the "commitment of marriage" before they have children' (p. 145).

There has also been a rise in people of the same gender choosing to live together within a loving relationship and adopting or having children of their own. Malmquist and Zetterqvist Nelson (2013) write that it is 'important to understand "family" as something that is continuously performed "doing family" – rather than a specific structure'.

Sobočan (2013) writes of Slovakian research carried out with families of the same gender who, despite deficient legislation and negative public approval of same-gender relationships, have tried to devise strategies to deal with homophobic attitudes to both parents and children.

With the introduction of the Equality Act in the UK in 2010, the country saw a bringing together of the Sex Discrimination Act (1975), Race Relations Act (1976) and the Disability Discrimination Act (1995). This meant that there could no longer be discrimination of people due to their faith, race/ethnicity and gender. The Act also prohibits 'direct discrimination' or 'victimisation' against any of the above groups of people and stipulates the need for early years settings to ensure that all children and families are valued and welcomed.

Despite these changes to family structures in the Western world, people living in other cultures in the developing world have different views on the role of the family, many of which may appear to those of us in the West to be quite outdated.

The family in the developing world

Bruner (2000), Rogoff (2003) and Smidt (2006) all espouse the need for practitioners to take into account the culture in which families live, stressing that even though families may have lived in the UK for many years there may still be areas and practices of their dominant culture that they may view as being important. Lindon (2012) shares this view and again accentuates the need for practitioners to discover in a sensitive way some of the practices and firmly held beliefs of families that might 'spill over' to the way they live. She continues to suggest that at times the way some families live may appear to those of us in the West as being old fashioned and represent the patriarchal society of days gone by (Burman 2010). However, it is important to recognise that children cope well with these differences in their cultural worlds and, rather than criticising them, practitioners should see them as different but not necessarily unusual (Smidt 2006).

In the developing world the role of the family may be very different to the West. It is common for families to be grouped as in the West but in other areas of the world the role of bringing up children can be very different. In the previous chapter I discussed the African view that 'it takes a village to raise a child'. Thus suggesting that childcare is not entirely reliant on families alone but others within the community. Bruner (2000) suggests that what is important for a child is the 'sustained and extended interaction with a committed and enculturated caregiver' (p. 6). He makes no suggestion as to who that person may be. He goes on to propose that while bringing up children is universal, the methods are often related to cultural views, belief systems or 'mythic representations'.

Consideration needs to be made that in many areas of the developing world pregnancy and childbirth can be dangerous. A woman growing up in the developing world may not have access to medical resources as in the West, therefore making infant mortality a possibility. A woman may progress through pregnancy but then not have enough food to adequately feed the baby themselves (DeLoache and Gottileb 2000). This can also result in mothers turning to formula milk, which can then cause issues because of dirty water in more remote places.

As was pointed out in the previous chapter, other cultures' interest in faith and spirituality can often be far more important than it is to many families in the West. Parents will often expect their children to grow up sharing 'deeply held views and beliefs around faith', something that I experienced when I visited Ghana a few years ago.

Case study 5.1

During a visit to Ghana with a group of 20 students who were all studying a degree in early childhood studies, the students shared an activity with practitioners where they were provided with empty water bottles, newspapers, tape and card and were asked to make props that could be used to tell a story to young children. To both my and the students' amazement many of the props made related to bible stories, which the practitioners then went on to retell using the props. The practitioners talked to the students and were amazed to hear that many of the students did not have any interest in any one particular faith.

The next day the students started volunteering in a number of preschools, nurseries and schools in a semi-rural area and were amazed that although the classrooms were very austere compared with those in the UK, there were a lot of bible-based posters and pictures around the room. Also, before lunch the children said Grace – a prayer thanking God for the food that they were about to eat – and then at the end of the day another prayer was said asking for blessing as the children returned to their homes.

Reflection

- Have you ever seen anything like this in practice?

- What is your view on this?

- What are some of the challenges that this practice could bring with it?

Another area of concern for countries in the developing world is famine, war and political unrest. Recently, newspapers and the media have been full of pictures of families fleeing their countries of origin in boats crossing the Mediterranean to various parts of Europe. As reported by Peck (2017), in the UK there are differing views on whether or not the country is too full to take families from some of these countries. However, the United Nations Refugee Council (UNRC) (2017) has announced that the refugee crisis is a state of emergency. This situation will inevitably have an impact on education in the West. Traumatised families and children may not only have seen war first hand, but will also have spent days and months travelling. Then when they arrive in Europe and settle here they will join schools in the West and unfortunately may experience racism from those in the communities who would prefer them not to be there (UNRC 2017). They may know nothing about the country's educational systems and expectations, may not speak the dominant language in the country and may have emotional issues brought about by the traumas they have experienced. Therefore practitioners need to have an awareness of the best way to support families in a compassionate way, ensuring that they are empowered rather than damaged by what they have been through (Williams 2008).

Terminology

Whenever issues are raised around people coming to the West, particularly to the UK, many different words are used to describe these people, this next part of the chapter will seek to describe what these words are and unpick their true meaning.

What is an immigrant?

An immigrant is a person who moves to live permanently in a different country. They do not leave their countries of origin because of war or persecution but to move nearer to family, to gain work or to seek a 'better' life. Currently in the UK there are discussions going on in relation to whether or not the UK has taken in too many families from other countries and whether this leads to areas that become like 'ghettos' where families from elsewhere in the world choose to live in social isolation (Chanda-Gool and Andrews 2017). Immigrants, unlike refugees and asylum seekers, have the correct paperwork required to move to another country and can move back to their countries of origin whenever they like (Macblain, Dunn and Luke 2017).

What is a refugee?

Refugees are people who have been forced to leave their home countries due to war, persecution or because of natural disaster. Very often they are highly skilled professionals in their country of origin yet when they arrive in the UK they appear to be stripped of all their rights and are often housed in the most deprived areas. Because of this they are often very resilient and have many skills and strengths to use in everyday life (Social Care Institute for Excellence 2015). Refugees are protected through international law such as the Refugee Convention (UNRA 1951) and once given 'leave to remain' in the UK are able to access the same services as UK nationals. Higgins (2017) suggests that throughout the world there are currently over 7 million children living as refugees, many of whom have seen conflict in their country of origin, which inevitably takes a severe emotional toll on them.

Over the years orphaned children have travelled to the UK and been supported by British charities such as Save the Children. Some children who seek refuge in the UK are victims of human trafficking whereby they are forced into slavery across the world and here in the UK. These children may be encouraged into forced marriages, servitude, forced labour in agriculture and factories or into crime (NSPCC n.d.). It is not unusual for refugees to be housed in many different places before settling in some of the larger cities across the UK.

What is an asylum seeker?

An asylum seeker is someone who comes to the UK from their home country for the same reasons as refugees but has not yet been granted leave to remain. Asylum seekers have fewer rights than refugees and are given just £35 a week for food, shelter and clothes in the UK whereas in other European countries they are given £50 a week. Permission to work in the UK is not given until asylum seekers have lived in the UK for over a year thus meaning that some go into illegal work purely because they cannot live on the amount given by the UK government (Amnesty International 2015).

In 2016 a report carried out for the National Children's Bureau (Renton, Hamblin and Clements 2016) suggested that despite the Healthy Child programme (Department of Health 2009), which sets out to improve the well-being of young children in an integrated way, vulnerable refugees and asylum seekers are still being 'barred' from health services. The report goes on to propose that the mental health of young refugees and asylum seekers is a huge issue, suggesting that they are 'particularly vulnerable to post traumatic stress, depression and anxiety' (p. 8), which is not surprising considering what some of these young children must witness before coming to the UK. The report suggested that although some areas of the UK are working hard to support families and ensure that they have access to services to support children's mental health, this is not the case in all areas of the UK.

Case study 5.2

Rosa and Derek came to the UK from Kosovo in 2008. Some members of their family had been murdered and so it was unsafe for them to remain in their home country. They had a little boy called Ernaud who, at that time, was 7 years old. Rosa was pregnant with her second child who was born in late 2008.

Ernaud struggled with school when he first arrived in the UK. He seemed to quickly pick up the language but seemed very sad, withdrawn and unhappy. The school was used to accepting child refugees and asylum seekers and had a mentoring scheme where a past refugee would mentor a newly arrived child. However, even with this support Ernaud seemed constantly distressed. The school asked one of their Kosovan bilingual support workers to spend some time working with Ernaud – she soon discovered that he had witnessed the murder of his uncle and was under-standably quite distraught about this. The school managed to get some support from the Children's and Adolescent Mental Health Association (CAMS), which helped Ernaud to come to terms with what he had witnessed. The organisation also worked alongside his parents and supported them to help Ernaud.

Reflection

- How would you work with a child who arrived in your setting as an asylum seeker?

- How do you support new families who come to your setting from other cultures?

- Do you know of local support agencies in your area that you could signpost families too?

What is cultural intelligence?

Earley and Wski (2004) suggest that cultural intelligence (CQ) is the ability of someone to be aware of the cultural code by which individuals and communities live and work. When the term 'intelligence' is used it is often linked with how clever and knowledgeable a person is. But here, as with emotional intelligence which is about being alert to others' emotional feelings (Goleman 1996), it reflects the ability of a person to understand and acknowledge that the role of culture is vital to how people come together and live their lives. It demonstrates an ability that someone has to be able to 'tease out' a group's behaviour and features and align them to their culture.

According to Otaigbe (2016), the term 'cultural intelligence' first became popular when it was used in the business world to try and understand the global workplace. He reports that according to the Cultural Intelligence Centre there are four main components of CQ. These are as follows:

- *Drive* – the determination to find out about other cultures.

- *Knowledge* – a person's ability to find out about and understand how cultures and communities live.

- *Strategy* – the ability to look at the ethos of an organisation and to consider it through a cultural lens – which could mean adapting it in order to make it more multicultural.

- *Action* – to do things to support families and communities while respecting their difference and diversity.

The National Association of Social Workers (2001) suggests that cultural intelligence is 'the process by which individuals and systems respond respectfully and effectively to people of all cultures . . . In a manner that recognises, affirms and values the worth of individuals, families and communities' (p. 11).

Dean (2001) describes CQ as a skill that is vital in the world of social work when professionals need some understanding of why it is that certain communities struggle to follow the practice and rules of a particular country.

Case study 5.3

A couple moved to the UK from India because they wanted a better life with more job prospects and their children to be educated in the UK. The mother gave birth to twins around two years after moving here. They didn't have a lot of money as the father could only find work in a pizza shop and they were living in rented accommodation. When the lady came to leave hospital after the birth of the children she was told by the hospital that she could not leave until she had got baby seats to take them home in – the couple did not have a car so did not need said baby seats and so she had to borrow two from friends.

The midwife visited and was alarmed to see that the couple only had a couple of moses baskets to put the children in – when she asked where the cot was the mother told her that in India it was customary for babies to co-sleep with their mother and father. However, this is not usually thought of as being good practice in the UK (Unicef 2017), so the couple chose to buy one cot and put both babies in the one cot.

Here we see an example of a family receiving advice because of different practices in the UK to those in India. Cultural intelligence is about using the lens of culture to understand the needs of families and children.

Reflection

- In your practice have you seen evidence of families from different cultures wanting to bring their children up differently to those from the UK?

- How would you deal with an issue like this in a sensitive manner?

- What could your setting do to enable families from other cultures to have a greater understanding of practices in the UK?

Crowne (2008) suggests that for people to become truly culturally intelligent they need a level of exposure to working with families and a propensity to investigate and experience the cultures of others and why their lives and traditions are different. The opportunity to become more culturally intelligent can be established first by becoming interested in the way families live and the differences in communities – this can be done by visits, conversations and a genuine interest to find out how other people live their lives. It may begin through travel to different countries and the opportunity to spend time living in communities that are different from your own. Rogoff (2003) believes that the only true way to get to know a community is to live within it, getting accustomed to their values and traditions and respecting differences.

Cultural intelligence is also about recognising the cultural tools that were discussed in Chapter 3 and also noticing cultural cues that may be different to how the dominant culture behaves. An example of this might be eating a meal. For most people in the West this is about eating with a knife and fork, sitting around a large table and talking to one another as we eat. However, in Asian countries families tend to sit on the floor around a low table and eat with their fingers. In China and Japan chopsticks are used. These are just some of the cues around eating – being culturally intelligent means that a person does not think of any of these practices as being superior to another.

Of course being truly culturally intelligent goes much deeper than just eating habits – it is about valuing all people, showing them respect and ensuring that we understand why it is that they may have different views to ours.

Reflection points

- Could the concept of cultural intelligence be used in your setting?

- In what way do you think it might assist you when working with families?

Policy requirements relating to working in partnership with families

As with all areas of early years practice, policy documents suggest that practitioners support the need for partnerships with parents and families relating to cultural diversity.

The Children and Families Act became statute in 2014 and introduced new requirements particularly around the safeguarding of young children. The Act set out to:

- protect young children through the adoption process;

- establish requirements relating to childcare;

- introduce new requirements through the new Special Educational Needs (SEN) Code of Practice 2014;

- introduce new legislation around the care process;

- introduce legislation around the rights of parents, particularly fathers.

Changes to this legislation have been problematic, particularly in response to the adoption of children who are from or have birth parents from other cultures. Before the introduction of this Act, children from other cultures were, where possible, placed for adoption with parents of a similar culture. However, the introduction of this Act dissolves this requirement in a move to speed up the adoption process, a shift that has been criticised by Muir (2010), who stresses that the move to ensure that potential parents are just 'sympathetic to and understand the issues to be confronted by a child of minority ethnic or mixed-race' could mean that children grow up to experience racism and discrimination. This is a view shared by Anderson (2014), who states that through the UN Convention on the Rights of the Child (UNICEF 1991), Articles 8 and 9 protect children and establish the need to recognise the importance of children having an identity, some of which is associated with their culture as we read in the previous chapter. Furthermore, Article 14 of the UNCRC dictates that children

> have the right to think and believe what they choose and also to practise their religion, as long as they are not stopping other people from enjoying their rights. Governments must respect the rights and responsibilities of parents to guide their child as they grow up.

This could be difficult if the child is brought up with a family who are of a different identity, colour or faith.

The Early Years Foundation Stage (EYFS)

As suggested in the introduction, the first EYFS written in 2008 by the Department for Children, Schools and Families stipulated the need for settings to work in close partnership with parents. It recognised, as did Bronfenbrenner, the centrality of the child and family within the microsystem and the need for settings to forge strong relationships with families. The EYFS then clearly set out the need for:

- two-way communication with parents as partners who really listen to each other, value each other's views and are prepared to work together to enable children to explore, grow and develop;

- sharing reciprocal information with each other relating to diet, behaviour, medical needs, languages spoken in setting, abilities or disabilities of the child and engage collaboratively in multi-agency working;

- discovering a child's likes and fascinations so that they can be encouraged in both the setting and the home;

- establishing the role of the key worker, who can help to bridge the gap between home and nursery and then nursery and school.

The most recent issue of the Early Years Foundation Stage (2017) continues to stipulate the importance of working alongside parents. However, in point 1.7 there is mention of the need to work closely with parents when children are bilingual. It discusses the need for children to first become literate in their home language before they are able to learn a new language. However, for some parents this proves a little controversial. Barley (2014) discusses how Somalian families view English as being far more important for their children to learn than their home language. She goes on to speak of the difficulties for children whose family language is different when they come to a school that primarily uses English as its dominant language. As a result of this a school in the north of the country that has a high level of children attending with English as an additional language is adjusting their curriculum to ensure that white children learn Somalian to help support children from that country. The DCSF, however, state that 'Bilingualism is an asset, and the first language has a continuing and significant role in identity, learning and the acquisition of additional languages' (2007, p. 4).

However, Issa and Hatt (2013) acknowledge that for some families it is essential that children should retain their home language and learn English alongside that language. They discuss the importance of practitioners who value all areas of children's lives and value the role of bilingual practitioners who can work with the whole family on an equal footing to ensure that family languages are celebrated and affirmed while children also learn English.

Rix (2011) describes the importance of bilingual workers in settings who are able to support children with their home languages with the following. A bilingual child from Somalia is silent in class. She is very serious and tends to distance herself from children in the class. However, when the Somalian teaching assistant comes into the class her behaviour changes. She is able to converse with the assistant and becomes happy and content. Parke et al. (2002) describe the situation of a child from Pakistan who seemed aloof, self-sufficient and quite stubborn when she first started nursery in the UK. However, as soon as the bilingual worker worked with her the staff began to see a different side to the child as she could share her language with the worker. The bilingual worker was not only able to get to know the child but was also able to build a relationship with the child's parents, which made the transition from home to the setting much easier.

Reflection points

- How do you work with parents whose dominant language is not English?

- What services help you to communicate with them more effectively?

When parents and practitioners work alongside each other in a reciprocal and sensitive way conversations can address challenges and issues and, as in the aforementioned school, enable children to learn about differences and diversity in a positive way.

Another area of importance mentioned in the EYFS (DCSF 2007) is the role of the key person in the setting.

What is a key person?

According to the DCSF (2007) a key person is someone in an early years setting who helps parents and children to get to know and understand the setting that their children will enter. This may be done initially through a home visit or during visits to the setting of both the parent and child. The key person strives to build a strong, sensitive, reciprocal relationship with the family to ease the many transitions the child will be part of during the early years. The early years worker should try to bridge the gap for the child between the setting and home/family.

In settings that are situated in multicultural areas this person will often be bilingual and will have knowledge of many languages used in the community and setting. This obviously helps families to understand the many intricacies of the setting and can help families to understand a little about the English educational system. Devarakonda (2013) discusses how bilingual assistants have been employed in the UK since 1966 and continue to be a vital element of today's educational provision. She suggests that not only are bilingual workers essential to families in settings they are also crucial in ensuring that resources used in the setting reflect the needs of the communities in which they are placed by adding input to which type of books, art, dressing-up clothes, etc. are used in the settings.

The bilingual worker can also help to support children and families in terms of their emotional well-being. As said previously, children coming to the UK as asylum seekers have often seen many horrific things and this may affect their emotional well-being. It is vital that the key person is aware of some of the life history of families so that they can support them and, if needed, put them in touch with other services that might support them (Kirmayer *et al.* 2011; Ward 2009). However, one should acknowledge that there is great diversity within individual communities and so one should not make the assumption that because a community is made up mainly of parents from the black and minority ethnic community (BME) that they will all speak the same language and follow similar traditions (Ward 2009).

Safeguarding issues

As with other policies previously mentioned in this book, the government needs to ensure that every child is safe, has access to a range of services and is being brought up in a home where they are loved and free from any kind of abuse or risk. In the UK it is set out in many policy documents that it is a professional's job to ensure that children are protected and free from harm. Many policies relating to safeguarding stem from the Children Act (2006), which was the first of its kind and particularly related to early years practice. The Act introduced the following:

- the Early Years Foundation Stage curriculum;

- discussion of the need for all practitioners including local authority staff, practitioners, teachers, social workers and community workers to work closely together and to speak up if they have fears around the safeguarding of young children;

- the need to ensure the sharing of information between agencies if there are any concerns about children in their care;

- the need to protect children from any kind of maltreatment;

- the appointment of a children's commissioner, who seeks to raise the awareness of safeguarding and how it works – this person can also become involved in individual cases if there are wider implitions to public policy.

However, after a number of high-profile senior case reviews, which suggested that the culture of children needs closer examination (NSPCC 2014) the then Secretary for Education, Michael Gove requested a review of safeguarding policies and procedures conducted across the UK. The review was led by Professor Eileen Munro from the London School of Economic and Political Science. In her report, Munro (2011) makes some suggestions to practitioners in terms of how they can better support families. Some of her suggestions are as follows:

- the 'Working Together to Safeguard Children' introduced in 2006 should remain as the core guidance for practitioners to use when they have worries about a child or family;

- local safeguarding boards should ensure that representatives from all communities come together to provide leadership to organisations working together to safeguard children;

- early introduction and referral of the very youngest children whose development may seem delayed or families who may be struggling with childcare for various reasons, this should ideally be done through Sure Start children's centres;

- the process of referring families should become less bureaucratic;

- the child protection scheme should be child-centred – therefore putting the child at the centre of all services offered to them thus enabling them to have a voice that is listened to and believed;

- to 'recognise diversity and apply anti-discriminatory and anti-oppressive principles in practice' (p. 40);

- to ensure that social workers have a range of communication skills or access to translators to ensure the true voice of every child can be heard.

Here we start to see recognition of the fact that the UK Government acknowledges that families are different and may need staff to be aware of this when working with them. The National Society for the

Protection of Cruelty to Children (NSPCC 2014) acknowledge that practitioners working with children and families need to be aware of some of the faith and cultural traditions of families from across the world while ensuring that these do not put children at risk of harm. The NSPCC continue to suggest that the culture of a family can be used as an excuse both in terms of what the family tell a practitioner and for the practitioner to explain away practices being carried out with a child. This accentuates the need for all practitioners working with families to have some knowledge about the many parenting practices used in homes and the need for practitioners to receive training relating to multiculturalism. The NSPCC (2014) continue to suggest that:

> Assessment tools should be adapted to ensure cultural sensitivity based on knowledge and understanding. Assessments should explore the impact of a person's culture on their life, including: spiritual practices, rites/blessings, beliefs and practices surrounding life events, dietary restrictions, personal care, daily rituals, communication, social customs and attitudes to healthcare and support.

Another issue that families from other cultures face is the non-recognition of the many services open to families from different cultures. A family living in the developing world and coming to the UK will need to be informed of the services on offer in the UK as they may not have experienced health or education in their countries of origin. When carrying out research with asylum-seeking families, Burchill and Pevalin (2012) discovered that there was ineffective engagement between health visitors and families due to little understanding from the families of the nature of the National Health Service (NHS). There were also issues around 'health tourism' where asylum seekers were viewed by people as just coming to the UK to seek out medical provision. Leadbetter and Litosseliti (2014) discuss the difficulties for families from abroad accessing NHS services and suggest that this may be because of communication issues, language and cultural barriers, poor NHS links with community services and a lack of understanding of the health care system. They go on to suggest that while practice in some areas is good with the best examples of practice recognising the needs of different cultures, many are still lacking suggesting that staff need to develop cultural intelligence in order to understand the needs of families.

Conclusion

This chapter first considered the role of the family and how this has changed, particularly over the past 50 years. It has also discussed the importance of working alongside families in a sensitive way to support them in bringing up their children. There has been discussion about some of the challenges that families experience when moving around the world and the impact that this may have on how they parent their children.

Some of the terms that are particularly used by the media when relating to families coming to the UK have been discussed, including the term 'cultural intelligence' and how it can help to support practitioners working with families in understanding their traditions and beliefs. There has been explanation of some of the policy documents that relate to families and especially the importance of the key/bilingual worker in building up secure relationships with families.

The next chapter will talk about how practitioners can work with children to promote their knowledge about difference and diversity in a positive way.

Points to consider

- How well does your setting work with families?

- What strategies does your setting use to work more effectively with parents from other cultures?

- How could your setting become more family friendly?

Further reading

Chanda-Gool, S. and Andrews, M. (2017) Language, cultural identity and belonging. In Parker-Rees, R. and Leeson, C. (eds) *Early Childhood Studies: An Introduction to the Study of Children's Lives and Children's Worlds* (pp. 129–142). London: Sage.

Goh, M. (2012) Teaching with cultural intelligence: Developing multiculturally educated and globally engaged citizens. *Asia Pacific Journal of Education* 32: 1–14.

Williams, F. (2008) Empowering parents in improving services for young children. In Anning, A. and Ball, M. (eds) *Sure Start to Children's Centres* (pp. 394–404). London: Sage.

References

Amnesty International (2015) The truth about refugees. www.amnesty.org.uk/truth-about-refugees.

Anderson, M. (2014) Protecting the rights of indigenous and multicultural children and preserving their cultures in fostering and adoption. *Family Court Review* 52(1): 6–27.

Barley, R. (2014) *Identity and Social Interaction in a Multi-Ethnic Classroom*. London: Tufnell Press.

Bruner, J. (2000) Foreword. In DeLoache, J. and Gottlieb, A. (eds) *A World of Babies: Imagined Childcare for Seven Societies* (pp. 1–6). New York: Cambridge University Press.

Burchill, J. and Pevalin, D. (2012) Barriers to effective practice for health visitors working with asylum seekers and refugees. *Community Practitioner* 85(7): 20–23.

Burman, E. (2010) *Deconstructing Developmental Psychology* (2nd edition). London: Routledge.

Campbell-Barr, V., Georgeson, J. and Selbie, P. (2016) International perspectives on workforce philosophy and politics. In Campbell-Barr, V. and Georgeson, J. (eds) *International Perspectives on Early Years Workforce Development* (pp. 45–58). Plymouth: Critical Publishing.

Chanda-Gool, S. and Andrews, M. (2017) Language, cultural identity and belonging. In Parker-Rees, R. and Leeson, C. (eds) *Early Childhood Studies: An Introduction to the Study of Children's Lives and Children's Worlds* (pp. 129–142). London: Sage.

Chambers, J. (2012) *A Sociology of Family Life: Change and Diversity in Intimate Relations.* Cambridge: Polity Press.

Crowne, K.A. (2008) What leads to cultural intelligence? https://doi-org.lcproxy.shu.ac.uk/10.1016/j.bushor.2008.03.010.

Dean, R.G. (2001) The myth of cross-cultural competence. *Families in Society: The Journal of Contemporary Human Services* 82(6): 623–630.

DeLoache, J. and Gottlieb, A. (2000) *A World of Babies: Imagined Childcare for Seven Societies.* New York: Cambridge University Press.

Department for Children, Schools and Families (DCSF) (2007) *Supporting Children Learning English as an Additional Language.* Norwich: Crown Copyright.

DCSF (2008) *The Early Years Foundation Stage.* Nottingham: DCSF.

Department of Health (2009) *The Healthy Child Programme: Pregnancy and the First Five Years of Life.* London: Department of Health.

Devararkonda, C. (2013) *Diversity and Inclusion in Early Childhood: An Introduction.* London: Sage.

Earley, P.C and Wski, E.M. (2004) Cultural intelligence. *Harvard Business Review* 82(10): 139–146.

Flandrin, L. (1979) *Families in Former Times.* Cambridge: Cambridge University Press.

Goleman, D. (1996) *Emotional Intelligence: Why It Can Matter More Than IQ.* London: Bloomsbury.

Greer, G. (1970) *The Female Eunuch.* London: Harper Collins.

Higgins, V. (2017) Children's well-being in the majority world: Developing sustainable life patterns. In Parker-Rees, R. and Leeson, C. (eds) *Early Childhood Studies: An Introduction to the Study of Children's Lives and Children's Worlds.* London: Sage.

Her Majesty's Stationery Office (HMSO) (2010) *The Equality Act.* London: HMSO.

HMSO (2017) *The Early Years Foundation Stage.* London: HMSO. www.gov.uk/government/publications.

Issa, T. and Hatt, A. (2013) *Language, Culture and Identity in the Early Years*. London: Bloomsbury.

Kirmayer, L.J., Narasiah, L., Munoz, M., Rashid, M., Ryder, A.G., Guzder, J., Hassan, G., Rousseau, C. and Pottie, K. (2011) Common mental health problems in immigrants and refugees: General approach in primary care. *Canadian Medical Association Journal* 183(12): 959–967.

Leadbetter, C. and Litosseliti, L. (2014) The importance of cultural competence for speech and language therapists. *Journal of International Research in Communication* 5(1): 1–26.

Lewis, J. (2001) *The End of Marriage: Individualism and Intimate Relations*. Cheltenham: Edward Elgar.

Lindon, J. (2012) *Equality and Inclusion in Early Childhood* (2nd edition). London: Hodder.

Macblain, S., Dunn, J. and Luke, I. (2017) *Contemporary Childhood*. Sage: London.

Malmquist, A. and Zetterqvist, K. (2013) Gay and lesbian parents. *Oxford Bibliographies*. www.oxfordbibliographies.com/.

Muir, H. (3 November 2010) The truth about inter-racial adoption. *Guardian*. www.theguardian.com/society/2010/nov/03/inter-racial-adoption.

Munro, E. (2011) The Munro review of child protection. *Interim Report: The Child's Journey*. www.nationalarchives.gov.uk.

National Association of Social Workers (NASW) (2001) *NASW Standards for Cultural Competency in Social Work Practice*. Washington DC: Author. www.socialworkers.org/practice/standards/NASWCulturalStandards.pdf.

National Society for the Prevention and Cruelty to Children (NSPCC) (n.d.) Child trafficking: What is child trafficking? www.nspcc.org.uk/preventing-abuse/child-abuse-and-neglect/child-trafficking.

NSPCC (2014) Culture and faith: Learning from case reviews. *Summary of Risk Factors and Learning for Improved Practice Around Culture and Faith*. www.nspcc.org.uk/preventing-abuse/child-protection-system/case-reviews/learning/culture-faith.

Office for National Statistics (2013) Women in the labour market. www.ons.gov.uk/employmentandlabourmarket/peopleinwork/employmentandemployeetypes/articles/womeninthelabourmarket/2013-09-25.

Otaigbe, O.O. (2016) *Building Cultural Intelligence in Church and Ministry*. London: Authorhouse.

Parke, T., Drury, R., Kenner, C. and Helvaara Robertson, L. (2002) Revealing invisible worlds: Connecting the mainstream with bilingual children's home and community learning. *Journal of Early Childhood Literacy* 2(2): 195–220.

Parsons, T. (1971) The normal American family. In Adams, B and Weirath, T. (eds) *Readings on the Sociology of the Family* (pp. 53–66). Chicago: Markham.

Peck, T. (8 February 2017) Government backtracks on pledge to take child refugees. *Independent*. www.independent.co.uk/news/only-350-syrian-refugee-children-will-be-allowed-to-settle-in-britain-thousands-less-than-promised.

Renton, Z., Hamblin, E. and Clements, K. (2016) *Delivering the Healthy Child Programme for Young Refugee and Migrant Children*. London: National Children's Bureau.

Rix, J. (2011) What's your attitude? Inclusion and early years settings. In Paige-Smith, A. and Craft, A. (eds) *Developing Reflective Practice in the Early Years* (2nd edition). Berkshire: Open University Press.

Rogoff, B. (2003) *The Cultural Nature of Human Development*. New York: Oxford University Press.

Shorter, E. (1975) *The Making of the Modern Family*. London: Fontana/Collins.

Smidt, S. (2006) *The Developing Child in the 21st Century*. London: Routledge.

Sobočan, A. (2013) Two dads/two moms: Defying and affirming the mom-dad family. The case of same-gender families in Slovenia. *Confero Essays on Education, Philosophy and Politics* 1: 90–122.

Social Care Institute for Excellence (2015) *Good Practice in Social Care for Refugees and Asylum Seekers*. London: Social Care Institute for Excellence.

Stone, L. (1977) *The Family, Sea and Marriage in England 1500–1800*. London: Weidenfield & Nicholson.

Unicef (1991) UN Convention on the Rights of the Child. www.unicef.org.uk/what-we-do/un-convention-child-rights.

Unicef (2017) Supporting child refugees across Europe. www.unicef.org.uk/child-refugees-europe.

The United Nations Refugee Council (UNCRC) (2017) History of the UNCRC. www.unhcr.org/uk/.

Ward, U. (2009) *Working with Parents in Early Years Settings*. Exeter: Learning Matters.

Weinberger, J., Pickstone, C. and Hannon, P. (eds) (2005) *Learning from Sure Start: Working with Young Children and Their Families*. Berkshire: Open University Press.

Williams, F. (2008) *Empowering Parents in Improving Services for Young Children*. In Anning, A. and Ball, M. (eds) *Sure Start to Children's Centres* (pp. 394–404). London: Sage.

6 Working with young children

Introduction

This chapter focuses on the need for practitioners to observe and reflect on some of the benefits and challenges of working with young children from other cultures. As has been suggested throughout this book, it is vital that children learn to acknowledge difference and diversity from birth. Yet as practitioners this can sometimes appear to be an impossible task. Maagero and Simonsen (2012) suggest that practitioners should use diversity as a resource rather than it being used as a way to sort or classify particular groups of children. This chapter will focus on particular areas of recommended practice that can be established to support all children and particularly those from other cultures.

The need to establish an 'enabling environment' (DFE 2008) will be discussed as, according to Fleer and Raban (2007) and Broadhead and Burt (2012), children pick up 'cues' from the environment within the 'context of everyday practice' (Fleer and Raban 2007, p. 105). They suggest that the environment should support children, whether or not they are able to communicate orally, with the activities that they choose to engage with. The importance of communication to young children will be discussed as well as recognition of the role of agency and participation in children's lives.

There will then be discussion about the importance of communication in early years settings, which will include a section relating to augmentative communication strategies and particularly the use of

Makaton, which Mistry and Barnes (2013) suggest can be useful for all children – therefore making it an inclusive tool.

The final section will discuss practice around bilingualism as this can be something of an emotive subject particularly if, as Hu, Torr and Whiteman (2014) identify, parents would prefer their children to speak English in their early years setting rather than the language spoken at home. Tobin, Arzubiaga and Adair (2013) discuss the ambiguities that can arise when practitioners feel that their own codes of practice are being challenged by parents who would prefer practice to be different. Suggesting that practitioners may be: 'unwilling to accommodate parents' wishes' in terms of issues such as bilingualism (p. 12).

An enabling environment

Chapter 3 discussed theorists' views on the role of the environment in children's play and the need for settings to represent different cultures within the environment. It introduced the view that particularly in the area of role-play it is vital that tools from other cultures are available and that dressing-up clothes, toys and books are available that represent more than just the dominant culture.

The concept of the 'enabling environment' was first adopted in the Early Years Foundation Stage, which was established by the Department for Children, Schools and Families (DCSF) in 2008. Like the focus on the 'unique child', the emphasis on the enabling environment has been maintained through each redevelopment of the document. Through research carried out in 2010, Grant and Mistry discovered that effective role-play environments can be particularly effective for children who speak English as an additional language. This is due to the opportunities the environment provides to develop children's listening and speaking skills. The enabling environment ensures that children receive 'experiences which respond to their particular needs' (p. 6) and as Luff (2012, p. 145) suggests should also be individualised through offering children 'open-ended resources' that enable them to explore, dictate and create their own play environment.

However, Smidt (2006) poses the challenge that enabling environments may be another Western notion, similar to the dichotomy of play-based learning suggested by Brooker (2002) in Chapter 3, that may be a 'damaging misconception' (p. 128) created by Western, middle-class assumptions. In the developing world there are very different environments for learning, many of which are not full of expensive toys and equipment as may be seen in the Western world. Instead they may be full of other types of cultural tools that are important to the child in their cultural context. Wood and Chesworth (2017) pose the view that good quality environments should support a child's ability to explore and learn and that they should be inclusive to all children.

Case study 6.1

A few years ago a nursery environment was set up in a Sure Start programme in a deprived area of the Midlands. The community was full of families from a range of different cultures and there were many children in the area that had special needs and a lot for whom English was an additional language (EAL). The centre had been created from an old shop that had been a much-loved part of the community.

During the building of the centre many families had given their views as to what the centre should look like and so the bottom floor became the community café and nursery with the offices upstairs for the multi-agency professionals working from the centre.

The nursery team and portage workers were given the job of creating the nursery and equipping it. Because of the needs of the children it had to be a fully inclusive area where there were not just a range of resources and equipment but also that space was created to ensure that areas were calm, comfortable and accessible for all.

The usual areas were important, such as the home and book corner, which were equipped with resources that met the cultural needs of the children. Books such as *Handa's Surprise* were used and it was ensured that the books represented the different cultural groups that were living in the area. Clothes and pieces of cloth from local shops were used as dressing-up clothes so that the children could choose what and how to wear the materials.

The mark-making and creative areas were full of different cultural tools, which again represented the cultures in the area. Not just pens and pencils but twigs were important. At times mud and water was provided so that children could make marks on paper. The outdoor space had wooden equipment as well as lots of balls for children to use. Over the years an area was established to enable parents, and particularly grandparents, to be involved with growing fruits and vegetables alongside the children – the produce was then used in the community café.

There was also an area that had a selection of large cardboard boxes. Beside them were large crayons and sometimes paints for the children to use on the boxes. These also supported children on the autistic spectrum who had a place to go if they were feeling nervous or scared. The area was closely monitored by adults.

- How could you make the environment in your setting more inclusive?

- What could you add to the environment in order that it is inclusive for all children?

What is meant by open-ended resources?

'Open-ended resources' is a term used widely in early years practice and it refers to equipment that is offered to children that they can do anything with. Sand and water are perhaps the most well known of these. However, more recently treasure baskets and heuristic play have become popular particularly for babies and younger children as they help to develop sensory skills (Featherstone 2013). With older children the term 'loose parts' has recently become popular. These too refer to natural resources, which are preferable to use for young children's play as they offer far more breadth and opportunity than plastic mass-produced toys.

Community Playthings (2015, p. 1) describe loose parts as being about 'alluring, beautiful and found objects and materials that children can move, manipulate, control and change through their play. Children can carry, design, line them up, take them apart and put them back together again in endless ways.'

These kinds of resources enable children to dictate the nature of their play and can support practitioners to introduce to children resources from other cultures. These may include cloth, books, different types of writing and prints, artefacts and pictures from other cultures. All of these ensure, as Baldock (2010) recommends, that children experience difference in a positive way with a variety of resources.

The value of outdoors

The case study discussed how parents, grandparents and professionals acknowledged the role of the outdoors in the lives of their children/ grandchildren. In recent years practice in the UK has shifted monumentally in terms of a greater interest in the outdoor environment and its ability to offer a different experience for children's exploration and learning. However, it is important to note that this is not a new concept. As reported by Hallowes (2015), the McMillan sisters pioneered an interest in the outdoors in their nurseries in the early eighteenth century, stating that 'once in the nursery the child comes under the influence of the great healers, earth, sun, air, sleep and joy'.

Recently the outdoors has been recognised as being an essential component to a child's health, especially in light of current concerns around child obesity (Ellaway *et al.* 2006) and in respect of the emotional well-being of young children (Knight 2009). Knight (2012) goes on to suggest that the decline of children playing outside may be partly due to the increase in the importance of technology and children's freedom to play with tablets and computer games as well as an interest in TV and the numerous channels available to young children.

However, if one turns to the curriculum in other areas of the world it is interesting that different environments such as the Reggio Emilia programme in Italy and the emerging interest in Forest Schools that has come from Scandinavian countries postulate the importance of the outdoors in all areas of children's lives. Papatheodorou and Moyles (2012, p. 13) suggest that outdoor play is the 'right of all children' in order to promote holistic well-being as well as to encourage play to enable all children to be 'capable learners'. Gandini (1998) refers to the environment as being the third teacher in a child's education.

Using cultural diversity as a resource

In New Zealand the Te Whariki curriculum, which is built on Bruner's sociocultural theory, endorses the view that

> learning leads development and occurs in relationships with people, places and things, mediated by participation in valued social and cultural activities. Play is an important means by which children try out new roles and identities as they interact with others. Peers provide forms of guidance and support.
>
> (MoE New Zealand 2003, p. 44)

It goes on to recognise that children are, as in the UK, acknowledged as being strong, confident and capable but they also focus on children's 'identity, language and culture' as constituting an essential part of their lives (p. 2). Like the UK, New Zealand has a long history of multiculturalism and the Te Whariki curriculum sees this as part of their work in 'emphasising children's bicultural foundation, our multicultural present and the shared future we are creating' (p. 2).

They view children as 'global citizens in a rapidly changing and increasingly connected world' (p. 2), thus recognising that children growing up in the twenty-first century are in a world where they are learning alongside children from other cultures and in a world where children have more opportunities to travel. This seems to accentuate more than the EYFS does the importance of the culture and heritage of all children. At the heart of this curriculum is the idea of a woven mat. Within this mat the following are vital to children:

- their sense of *well-being*;

- *belonging* to the community of both the setting and their home;

- the *contribution* that children make in the setting and their community;

- the way that children *communicate*;

- children's *exploration* and learning.

Weaving throughout these elements is the new life and growth that happens while children are attending the setting. Another strand of the mat relates to:

- the *holistic* development of children;

- the sense of *empowerment* when children achieve;

- the development and importance of *family and community* within the setting.

An entire section of their curriculum relates to the child's identity, culture and language, recognising that these are a vital element of their worlds. It would be good to see the UK recognising this more fully. Through this curriculum it can be acknowledged that all children have an identity, a culture and a language but how much is this valued in the UK? Here we can acknowledge greater evidence of children growing up knowing who they are, recognising their cultural heritage and recognising the role of communication, but how can this be done with children in an open way?

Activities that can support difference and diversity

In Chapter 1, I spoke about the significance of inclusion as a whole-team approach and the importance of activities reflecting not just the dominant culture of the setting. To try and engage children in conversations about difference is a very positive thing and Baldock (2010) reiterates the need also for craft, dressing-up activities, books, food and singing activities to represent a range of cultures. Recently a child had a lovely painting on the outside of her bedroom door. It was a portrait of her, in which she had painted her hair blonde. At the bottom of the picture was a quote from the child, which said 'I am different because I have got blonde hair' (see Figure 6.1). In a very gentle way the children in the nursery had started to discuss difference in a positive way. These kinds of activities are a positive way of encouraging practitioners to embrace difference and diversity.

Another way of recognising difference and diversity is through communication and teaching children songs in other languages. Leverett

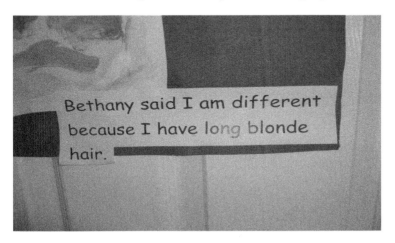

Figure 6.1 Using cultural diversity as a resource

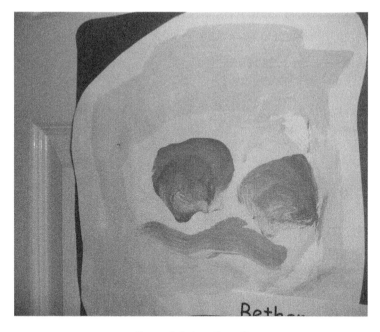

Figure 6.1 (continued)

(2008) suggests the benefits of family books that are made with photographs of the family and some explanation of the ways that they live and the children grow up. In the past I have used these not only with bilingual children to share with a larger group of children but also to encourage their communication skills.

Reflection points

- Is it common practice in your setting for you to plan around children's identity and culture?

- What activities can you introduce that encourage children to see themselves as unique?

The importance of communication in the early years

It is also vital when considering the environment for learning that importance is placed on the role of communication. Children have the ability to communicate through many different forms – these could include:

- speech;
- signs;
- eye gaze/pointing;
- body language;
- drawing;
- writing;
- storying;
- augmentative communication systems such as picture exchange communication systems (PECS) or through technology.

It is important to acknowledge here, as does Rinaldi (2005), that children have a 'hundred languages' that they use to communicate both with themselves, each other and adults.

Recently Lancaster and Broadbent (2003) orchestrated RAMPS, which is a tool used to stimulate reflection within a team relating to how well the environment is set up to listen to children. RAMPS stands for:

- **R** – the *recognition* of the many languages of children and the need for practitioners to identify that while most children will happily talk and engage with children and adults, some may find this more difficult and will choose different ways to communicate.

- **A** – *allocating* areas in the setting where children are able to converse. This is about ensuring that areas in the setting are set up to enable children to talk to each other. This could be a comfortable area similar to the book corner where there are cushions and where children can congregate and talk. Photographs on the walls of either the children or the community could be used to stimulate discussion.

- **M** – *making* time for children to communicate. This is about the need for practitioners to understand children's communication skills and to develop their practice giving children time to communicate. The Hanen Project (2016) discusses the need for practitioners to 'observe, wait and listen' for young children to communicate, thus enabling them to take the lead in conversation. It also suggests that when asking a child to do something that you give time to the child by counting to 10 in your head, before interceding to elaborate on what you have asked them. This suggests that children need time to communicate effectively.

- **P** – *providing* choice that enables children to make decisions and respects the need for them to do so. The more opportunity that children have to make their own choices the more they will see themselves as someone who has a voice and is not afraid to use it. In terms of early years practice this relates to the activities children are able to take part in, the food they can eat and the clothes they like to wear.

- **S** – *subscribing* to reflective practice, which enables practitioners to really think about the needs of children. Reflective practice is, as was pointed out in Chapter 1, a crucial tool for early years practitioners in allowing them to understand the needs of children and their uniqueness.

It is also important that children see examples of different kinds of communication in their setting. For children who are experiencing English as an additional language (EAL) this is vital. Galley (2015) promotes the view that inclusion is about offering children environments that are rich in different kinds of prints, whether this be text from a variety of cultures, as well as through drawings, photographs and symbols. Galley also raises the point that currently in the UK, 80 per cent of children enter school with 'impoverished speech and poor listening skills' (2015, p. 35). These environments need to ensure that children are encouraged to communicate through various different forms and that practitioners need to, in the words of Rinaldi (2005, p. 20), 'Listen to the hundred, the thousand languages, symbols and codes used to express ourselves and communicate, and with which life expresses itself and communicates to those who know how to listen'.

Reflection points

- How do practitioners in your setting ensure that the voice of the child can be heard in different ways?

- How do you ensure that children are given the time to communicate in meaningful ways?

- How do you ensure that children are able to make choices in issues that affect them?

Agency

'Agency' is a term that is used particularly when focusing on children as democratic individuals who should be enabled to have a voice in all areas of their lives. The term particularly reflects Article 12 of the UN Convention of the Rights of the Child (Unicef 1990) which states all children have the right to 'express their views, feelings and wishes in all matters affecting them, and to have their views considered and taken seriously'.

In 2015, Barr and Borkett suggest that the term 'agency' refers to a child's ability to have choice and their voice heard. They go on to suggest that in early years settings this may involve:

- having a say in which resources are set out;

- choosing what snack/meals they would like and being involved in the planning of menus;

- discussing how the setting should be involved in the community;
- being able to state what interests and fascinates them; and
- choosing books and Makaton signing during group times.

More recently Wood and Chesworth have suggested (2017) that children's agency is 'central to how they organise and develop their play with peers and with different materials' (p. 5).

Giving children these kinds of opportunities and choice is central in helping them to see themselves as democratic people whose voices should be heard. However, it is suggested by Barr and Borkett (2015) that while in schools children have the opportunity to be part of school councils, this happens less often in early years settings.

Cregan and Cuthbert (2014) suggest that the term 'agency' may differ depending on the culture that the child lives in. They suggest that for children growing up in the West, agency is the opportunity that children have to choose activities and to balance play and education, whereas for children growing up in the developing world they may need to be balancing paid work, the care of siblings, play, education and faith activities. These views support Macblain, Dunn and Luke's (2017) analysis that, particularly in the West, children are now recognised as 'social actors and informants in their own rights' (p. 30). They go on to suggest that children are no longer seen as silent in matters that affect them but are now seen as having the scope to understand and 'act on their world'. However, in research carried out between American and Nepalese children, Chernyak et al. (2013) suggest that while there are some clear differences between cultures around children's agency there are also some similarities. From their research they discovered that 'cultures do in fact differ in the extent to which children perceive and value choice in everyday contexts' (p. 1348).

This may relate to the fact that in the developed world children have access to far more resources than those in the developing world. However, Chernyak et al.'s research also indicated that, as with Hall's (2004) views about agency, it is also about a person's ability to behave with intent and an awareness of other people, suggesting that the term 'agency' also relates to one's responsibilities to others and society.

Reflection points

- Have you ever considered at what point you believe that children have 'agency' over their lives?

- Do you think that others working in your setting would have a different view? If so, why might this be?

- How do you give children in your setting agency over their lives?

- How could you encourage them to have more of a voice in the process of setting up the environment?

- What part does your setting play in having a voice within your local community?

Alongside the term 'agency', another word that is used particularly in terms of children having a voice is 'participation'.

What is meant by participation?

The term participation gained momentum when the Every Child Matters green paper was passed by New Labour in 2003. The paper was launched after the horrific murder of Victoria Climbié – a child who was raised by her Nigerian relatives in the UK and suffered shocking systematic abuse, eventually dying. After the Laming Report (Safeguarding Children 2009) issued investigations into both this and other murders of children by their parents, the Every Child Matters paper was launched in order to not just prevent child deaths, but also to ensure that a child's voice was heard more readily in all areas of their lives, especially in safeguarding procedures.

The term 'participation' relates to the need for the voice of the child to be heard and to ensure that children have more of a voice in issues that affect them. However, this is considered by some to be controversial. Macblain *et al.* (2017) point out that views around the voice of the child may differ depending on who is being consulted. They argue that some practitioners may struggle with the notion, suggesting that babies are not old enough to make big decisions in relation to their lives. MacNaughton, Rolfe and Siraj-Blatchford (2004) suggest that even though children are considered able to make their own decisions, that there is still 'contention' relating to children's 'meaningful participation' in issues that relate to them.

As with the term 'agency', it has been suggested that participation may be seen differently in different cultures. Nichols (2007) makes the point that while children are being viewed as 'young citizens' more and more, they cannot receive 'full social participation' until they leave school (p. 121). Edwards (2015) makes the case, as was suggested in Chapter 2, that participation and children's rights continue to be a 'Westernised' view, which cannot necessarily be embedded into the developing world because of the restrictions caused by a lack of resources and the differing views of adults in terms of children's rights.

Case study 6.2

A group of Somalian parents who had first come to the UK as asylum seekers but had since been given residency were planning to set up a parent and toddler group for other asylum-seeking families in the children's centre. Four of the mothers had arranged the necessities of where it would be held, the timing of the group, who would lead it and what the sessions would include. The parents were also informed by staff in the children's centre that they would need to attend safeguarding training as they would be in direct contact with adults and children. The plan was that, at the start of the group a member of the children's centre team should support the group but then that support would diminish as the group became more established.

The women chose to attend the training together and were somewhat alarmed by what they viewed as some of the 'rules and restrictions' mentioned in the training. They were unaware of the need to always have two adults in the room overseeing the care of children or the necessity of logging any tumbles or falls that the children may have.

The team planned that children should be offered a choice of food at snack time and be allowed to choose what they ate. They were also surprised how children were included in choosing songs at the end of each session. This was done with a prompt box, which included toys represented in the songs that the children chose.

This was all very different to education in Somalia, which was far more structured and as the parents saw it 'educational' and not so focused on giving the child a voice. However, over time the parents, with support of the team, started to see that there could be some shared understanding of the routines in the group.

The group continued to run for a further three years before it was felt that members of the group were ready to move to a larger group of parents and children. Two of those four mothers then went on to train as early years workers and to influence how cultures could come together sensitively and positively within the city.

Reflection

- How might you work with families from other cultures to share some of the safeguarding laws in the UK?

Kanyal and Gibbs (2014) go on to stress the importance of different approaches and strategies being used in practice to enable all children to have a voice and to be listened to. One such strategy that can be used is the Mosaic approach.

The Mosaic approach

The Mosaic approach was developed in London in 2001 by Clark and Moss and sought to give a voice to young children, particularly those who had special needs. The methodology, which was first developed for use in research, was adapted and is now used to enable children to have a voice through different mediums. The approach views the role of the child as being active in their own learning and exploration, using different tools to investigate their environments. Initially, it was used with respect to the outdoor environment but it is now used to evaluate all learning environments.

At the heart of the approach is the notion that all children have a voice and also have a right to participate and be active in their own lives, but that this may be demonstrated through different formats rather than just relying on speech. Like Rinaldi (2005), this approach recognises the different ways in which children communicate and suggests different methods to do this. It also emphasises that the approach can be adapted for all situations. The tools used within this methodology are able to be embedded into early years practice and would support all children, particularly those who might be bilingual.

The approach uses observations, child interviews, photographs, map making and tours of the setting, followed by focus groups to gain the child's and the adult's perspectives of an area (stage 1). Second, the data is discussed with all participants in a way that is acceptable to their needs (stage 2). The third stage views implementation of the information gained during the process. This then becomes part of a continual reflective cycle that makes changes to the environment and ways of working in the light of what the research discovers.

The use of augmentative communication strategies in early years settings

The term 'augmentative communication' refers to 'a set of tools and strategies that an individual uses to solve everyday communicative challenges' (Bailey 2016, p. 1). These can be strategies similar to those mentioned previously in the chapter and the term refers particularly to strategies such as Makaton signs and Rebus symbols, picture exchange communication systems (PECS) and electronic communication systems, which can be used by either touch or through eye gaze. These systems can help to develop children's communication skills, with most of them incorporating speech alongside signs and symbols. All of these strategies not only help children who have special needs but can also support bilingual children who are learning English alongside another language. Jonathan Bryan, a child with cerebral palsy and brain damage reports how he struggled to communicate at a young age and as a result spent much of his time in a special school, feeling frustrated because he was not able to communicate orally. Eventually his parents removed him from the special school and began to educate him at home. They slowly discovered that with the use of an 'eye-gaze' computer he was able to learn to read and subsequently communicate through the use of a computer mouse that worked when he looked at it. Bryan (2017) has since gone on to write a blog, which he uses to share his experience with other children with disabilities.

In 2013 ICAN reported that a million children across the UK struggle with their communication. In 2009 Hartshorne reported that 80 per cent of children enter school aged 5 with under-developed communication skills. Many of these children also have to cope with the additional challenge of learning English alongside the language that is used within their homes. Augmentative communication is especially helpful for such children.

One strategy that is highly recognised by many as being a useful tool is that of Makaton – a language programme designed by Mary Walker, a speech and language therapist, and Kathy Johnston in the 1970s. The system uses signs and symbols alongside the spoken word to encourage young children to communicate (Makaton.org n.d.). In 2004 I documented the usefulness of Makaton to support children who struggle to communicate through language (Borkett 2004). Signs that are similar to those used in British Sign Language are used alongside single words to encourage children to communicate. Symbols can be used alongside the signs to label equipment around the setting and also as headings for children's work and the two together can help to support children's language, communication and literacy skills.

Since the development of Makaton, Mistry and Barnes (2013) have carried out research in order to discover its effectiveness in supporting bilingual learners. Their research discovered that the use of Makaton in a reception class with children who had English as an additional language (EAL) seemed to indicate that Makaton supported them to learn English. They endorse the use of Makaton to support language acquisition first through non-verbal body language and communication behaviours that children pick up relatively easily, for instance, a wave for goodbye, shaking of the head for no, a thumbs-up as a positive gesture, thus ensuring that Makaton does not only recognise the use of signs but also the words that go alongside them. They went on to report that using Makaton also reduced anxiety for children who were unable to communicate effectively and gave evidence that the use of signing in this study 'increased the use of speech' (p. 607) with bilingual learners. This also had a benefit to the children's behaviour as they became less frustrated when they could communicate more effectively.

Health care professionals have also acknowledged the benefits of Makaton to support children and young people in health settings, with 80 per cent of nurses in one study viewing it as a vital tool to support their work with both children with special needs and bilingual learners (Vinales 2013).

It is vital that all children are encouraged to communicate to ensure that their needs are met in whatever way they find easiest.

Case study 6.3

Recently I accompanied a 5-year-old Polish boy called Ernauld on a trip to the park. Ernauld has severe learning needs and is unable to communicate orally. His parents have lived in the UK for four years and while they are picking up English well they use Polish to communicate at home.

Ernauld did not seem particularly interested by the animals that he saw while being pushed in his buggy but he loved feeling the hay in the stationary tractor. After dinner the children had some time in the park. By this time Ernauld was out of his buggy and so I followed his lead towards the swings. I put him in the swing and said 'Ready, steady, go' a couple of times. He laughed and smiled enthusiastically at being in the slide. After about four goes I wondered if I could encourage Ernauld to dictate when he wanted to be pushed. So rather than saying the word 'go', I encouraged Ernauld to communicate with me. The first couple of times he looked at me and then slowly he started to make a noise with a similar intonation as I had given. Although Ernauld's needs were profound he was still able to dictate some play within his day.

Reflection

- How do you enable children in your setting to have a voice?

- Do you purely rely on the voice for children to speak or do you use other methods to encourage them to communicate?

- What more could you do in your setting to enable children to have a voice?

Bilingualism and young children

A chapter that has focused on the voice of the child in a book about cultural diversity needs also to acknowledge some of the benefits and address some of the issues around bilingualism.

Bilingualism is the ability that a person has to speak more than one language (NALDIC 2011b). Soderman and Oshio (2008, p. 298) suggest that the ability for children to learn one language is complex and made up of different parts:

- *Phonology* – the sounds within a language, children are often involved in the learning of these through phonics teaching.

- *Vocabulary* – the words that make up the language.

- *Grammar* – the way that words are ordered and used.

- *Pragmatics* – the rules of how language is used.

Neaum (2012) suggests that children with English as an additional language (EAL) need to first come to know the language used widely in their family, before they then go on to use a new language that may be more prevalent in their early years setting. In 2007 the DCSF set out a publication particularly related to bilingualism (DCSF 2007), which shared a similar view to Neaum (2012) that 'a child's first language has a continuing and significant role in identity, learning and the acquisition of additional languages' (p. 4). Thus suggesting the benefits both of bilingualism and the importance for children to have their home language fully embedded before being able to take on a new language.

Barley (2014) suggests that children who have little English can struggle when coming into a setting that is 'predominantly English speaking' (p. 23), particularly if the child's family would prefer that the child speaks English while attending the setting. This view is substantiated by Tobin *et al.* (2013) who discovered through research carried out in Solano, California, that immigrant families would have preferred their children to just speak English in their setting.

Pim (2010) suggests that there are two types of bilingualism. First, a child who from birth is brought up with more than one language being used at home. Maybe a child whose mother is French and so uses this alongside the father's use of English. As the child grows up they will become used to both languages and be more likely to use them simultaneously from an early age. The second type of bilingualism relates to children who have learnt a language used in the home such as Mirapur or Pashti and then move into education in a setting that predominantly speaks only English. The DCSF stresses that it is possible for children to become 'conversationally fluent' (2007, p. 5) in one language in the first three years of life, but that it can then take up to five years to develop another language alongside the first.

Many authors document the view that children who are learning a new language alongside an existing one will go through a silent period where they are experiencing the confusion of a new language being all around them, yet they are returning home every day to use their home language (DCSF 2007; Galley 2015; Parke et al. 2002; Soderman and Oshio 2008). A period of acclimatisation is needed before the child will use either their home or new language independently. During this time the child may use play as a way of trying out both languages in a safe and enjoyable environment (NALDIC 2011a).

Another thing that bilingual people do is something called code-switching, which Akindele and Adegbite (2013) describe as the 'means of communication which involves a speaker alternating between one language and another in communicative events' (p. 92). This is a usual occurrence between bilingual people and if one is involved in a conversation with someone who is bilingual it can be observed regularly.

The DCSF (2007, p. 2) point out that often children learning English as an additional language are 'more vulnerable to poor outcomes' at the end of the Foundation Stage. This may be due to many factors, such as:

- families from other cultures living in some of the more disadvantaged communities;

- a lack of English-speaking role models in the home;

- practitioners who may not be aware of how to work with children who are bilingual.

Another issue that bilingual children have to contend with is carrying out the Early Years Foundation Stage assessment at the end of reception when they are assessed on their ability to:

- listen and pay attention;

- understand and follow instructions;

- speak.

All of these requirements could be a lot more difficult for a child who, as pointed out earlier, may take five years to become completely bilingual (DCSF 2007). Hood and Mitchell (2017) suggest that actions such as these only help to marginalise bilingual learners by giving them a different experience of education.

How can settings support bilingual children?

Much of what has already been written about in this chapter will support children who are learning an additional language but some particular strategies include:

- ensuring that the environment shows examples of art, music and books from other cultures and not just those from the dominant culture;

- recognising many of the cultural festivals that are celebrated across the world with children and families known to the setting;

- visiting areas and taking photographs of areas where there are large numbers of different cultures represented and using these photographs as a discussion resource;

employing bilingual workers as a vital resource to introduce different foods, stories, books and artefacts to the children and to forge positive open relationships with parents so that they feel comfortable to discuss their cultures and traditions with you in an atmosphere of interest and respect.

The importance of bilingual staff

Many of the references used in this section about bilingualism refer to the benefits of having bilingual staff in settings as key workers to support both children and their families. This support could be around cultural concerns about dress, food, language, traditions, faith and the differences in expectations of parents around education and their children. Parke *et al.* (2002) discuss the importance of bilingual workers who can understand children's languages and who are able to observe children and interpret their actions and play through dialogue in another language.

Conclusion

Through this chapter there has been discussion around the need to support children's learning through an 'enabling environment' that also values the need to recognise children as democratic people who have the right to make choices on matters that affect them. Two strategies known as RAMPS and the Mosaic approach have been introduced and the benefits of how they support staff and children evaluated. Augmentative communication systems have been discussed with particular focus on the role of Makaton alongside speech to help children to communicate. Finally, issues around some of the issues and challenges of bilingualism have been discussed.

The next chapter will draw the book to its conclusion while also recommending resources and strategies that can be used to support inclusive practice.

Points to consider

- How can you ensure that all children in your setting acknowledge difference and diversity?

- What activities could you plan that will do this?

- How can you support families to view both their home language and English as being a vital part of a child?

Further reading

Clark, A. and Moss, P. (2001) *The Mosaic Approach*. London: National Children's Bureau.

Galley, S. (2015) Creating an inclusive environment for supporting children with English as an additional language. In Brodie, K. and Savage, K. (eds) *Inclusion and Early Years Practice* (pp. 33–55). Oxon: David Fulton.

Gascoyne, S. (2016) *Sensory Play: Play in the EYFS*. London: Practical Preschool.

References

Akindele, F. and Adegbite, W. (1999) *The Sociology and Politics of English in Nigeria: An Introduction*. Nigeria: Obafemi Awolowo University Press.

Bailey, J. (2016) What is augmentative and alternative communication (AAC)? www.asha.org/public/speech/disorders/AAC/k.

Baldock, S. (2010) *Understanding Cultural Diversity in the Early Years*. London: Sage.

Barley, R. (2014) *Identity and Social Interaction in a Multi-Ethnic Classroom*. London: Tufnell Press.

Barr, K. and Borkett, P. (2015) Play with children from diverse cultures. In Moyes, J. (ed.) *The Excellence of Play* (pp. 275–285). Berkshire: Open University Press.

Borkett, P.A. (2004) Diversity and inclusion in the early years. In Kay, J. (ed.) *Good Practice in the Early Years* (pp. 91–115). London: Bloomsbury.

Broadhead, P. and Burt, A. (2012) *Understanding Young Children's Learning Through Play: Building Playful Pedagogies*. London: Routledge.

Brooker, L. (2002) *Starting School: Young Children Learning Cultures*. London: University of London.

Bryan, J. (22 January 2017) I talk with my eyes. *Guardian*. www.theguardian. com/lifeandstyle/2017/jan/27/experience-i-talk-with-my-eyes.

Chernyak, N., Kushnir, T., Sullivan, K.M. and Wang, Q. (2013) A comparison of American and Nepalese children's concept of freedom of choice and social constraint. *Journal of Cognitive Science* 37: 1345–1355.

Clark, A. and Moss, P. (2001) *The Mosaic Approach*. London: National Children's Bureau.

Community Playthings (2015) *Loose Parts: Inspiring Play in Young Children*. Minnesota: Red Leaf Press.

Cregan, K. and Cuthbert, D. (2014) *Global Childhoods: Issues and Debates*. London: Sage.

Department for Children, Schools and Families (DCSF) (2007) *Supporting Children Learning English as an Additional Language: Guidance for Practitioners in the Early Years Foundation Stage*. Norwich: Crown Copyright.

DCSF (2008) *The Early Years Foundation Stage*. Nottingham: DCSF.

Department for Education (DFE) (2003) Every Child Matters. www.education.gov.uk/consultations/downloadableDocs/EveryChildMatters.pdf.

Edwards, M. (2015) *Global Childhoods*. Northwich: Critical Publishing.

Ellaway, A., Kirk, A., Macintyre, S. and Muhries, N. (2006) Nowhere to play? The relationship between the location of outdoor areas and deprivation in Glasgow. *Health and Place* 13(2): 557–561.

Featherstone, S. (2013) *Treasure Baskets and Heuristic Play*. London: Bloomsbury.

Fleer, M. and Raban, B. (2007) Constructing cultural-historical tools for supporting young children's concept formation in early literacy and numeracy. *Early Years* 27(2): 103–118.

Galley, S. (2015) Creating an inclusive environment for supporting children with English as an additional language. In Brodie, K. and Savage, K. (eds) *Inclusion and Early Years Practice* (pp. 33–55). Oxon: David Fulton.

Gandini, L. (1998) Education and caring spaces. In Edwards, C., Gandini, L. and Forman, G. (eds) *The Hundred Languages of Children* (pp. 410–420). Greenwich, CT: Ablex.

Grant, K. and Mistry, M. (2010) How does the use of role-play affect the learning of year 4 children in a predominantly EAL class? *Education 3–13: International Journal of Primary, Elementary and Early Years Education* 38(2): 155–164.

Hall, D.E. (2004) *Subjectivity*. New York: Routledge.

Hallowes, A. (2015) History of the McMillan sisters. www.mcmillannursery school.co.uk/?p=2078.

The Hanen Project (2016) Communication development in pre-school children with language delays. www.hanen.org/Programs/For-Parents/ It-Takes-Two-to-Talk.asp.

Hartshorne, M. (2009) *The Cost to the Nation of Children's Poor Communication*. London: Routledge.

Hood, P. and Mitchell, H. (2017) Assessment and school readiness: Play and pedagogy. *BERA–TACTYC Early Childhood Research Review*. www.bera. ac.uk/.../bera-tactyc-early-childhood-research-review-2003-2017.

Hu, J., Torr, J. and Whiteman, B. (2014) 'Parents don't want their children to speak their home language': How do educators negotiate partnerships with Chinese parents regarding their children's use of home language and English in early childhood settings? *Early Years: An International Research Journal* 34(3): 255–270.

Kanyal, M. and Gibbs, J. (2014) Participation: Why and how? In Kanyal, M. (ed.) *Children's Rights 0–8. Promoting Participation in Education and Care* (pp. 45–62). London: Routledge.

Knight, S. (2009) *Forest Schools and Outdoor Learning in the Early Years*. London: Sage.

Knight, S. (2012) Valuing outdoor spaces: Different models of outdoor learning in the early years. In Papatheodorou, T. and Moyles, J. (eds) *Cross-Cultural Perspectives on Early Childhood*. London: Sage.

Lancaster, P and Broadbent, V. (2003) *Listening to Young Children*. Buckingham: Open University Press.

Leverett, S. (2008) Working with children and transitions. In Foley, P. and Leverett, S. (eds) *Connecting with Children: Developing Working Relationships*. Bristol: Open University Press.

Luff, P. (2012) Challenging assessment. In Papatheodorou, T. and Moyles, J. (eds) *Cross-Cultural Perspectives on Early Childhood*. London: Sage.

Maagero, E. and Simonsen, B. (2012) Constructing an inclusive culture in kindergartens. In Papatheodorou, T. and Moyles, J. (eds) *Cross-Cultural Perspectives on Early Childhood* (pp. 77–88). London: Sage.

Macblain, S., Dunn, J. and Luke, I. (2017) *Contemporary Childhood*. London: Sage.

MacNaughton, G., Rolfe, S.A. and Siraj-Blatchford, I. (eds) (2004) *Doing Early Childhood Research: International Perspectives on Theory and Practice*. Buckingham: Open University Press.

Makaton.org (n.d.) Let's talk Makaton: Makaton training. www.makaton.org/training/?gclid=EAIaIQobChMIw5bomau91QIVw7vtCh3I8QpdEAAYASA AEgleiPD_BwE.

Ministry of Education New Zealand (2003) *Characteristics of Professional Development Linked to Enhanced Pedagogy and Children's Learning in Early Childhood Settings*. Wellington, New Zealand: Ministry of Education.

Mistry, M. and Barnes, D. (2013) The use of Makaton for supporting talk, through play, for pupils who have English as an additional language. *Education 3–13: International Journal of Primary, Elementary and Early Years Education* 41(3): 603–616.

NALDIC (2011a) Stages of early bilingual learning. https://naldic.org.uk.

NALDIC (2011b) What is bilingualism? https://naldic.org.uk.

Neaum, S. (2012) *Language and Literacy for the Early Years*. London: Sage.

Nichols, S. (2007) Children as citizens: Literacies for social participation. *Early Years: An International Research Journal* 27(2): 119–130.

Papatheodorou, T. and Moyles, J. (eds) (2012) *Cross-Cultural Perspectives on Early Childhood*. London: Sage.

Parke, T., Drury, R., Kenner, C. and Robertson, L.H. (2002) Revealing invisible worlds: Connecting the mainstream with bilingual children's home and community learning. *Journal of Early Childhood Literacy* 2(2): 195–220.

Pim, C. (2010) *How to Support Children Learning English as an Additional Language*. Cheshire: LDA.

Rinaldi, C. (2005) Documentation and assessment: What is the relationship? In Clark, A., Kjorholt, A. and Moss, P. (eds) *Beyond Listening: Children's Perspectives on Early Childhood Services* (pp. 17–28). Bristol: The Policy Press.

Safeguarding Children Academy (2009) *Laming Report: Index of Recommendations*. www.safeguardingchildrenea.co.uk/resources/lord-laming-report-summary.

Smidt, S. (2006) *The Developing Child in the 21st Century: A Global Perspective on Child Development*. Oxon: Routledge.

Soderman, A.K. and Oshio, T. (2008) The social and cultural contexts of second language acquisition in young children. *European Early Childhood Education Research Journal* 16(3): 297–311.

Tobin, J., Arzubiaga, A.E. and Adair, J.K. (2013) *Children Crossing Borders: Immigrant and Teacher Perspectives on Pre School*. New York: Russell Sage Foundation.

Unicef (1990) UN Convention on the Rights of the Child. www.unicef.org.uk/what-we-do/un-convention-child-rights/.

Vinales, J. (2013) Evaluation of Makaton in practice by children's nursing student. *Nursing Children and Young People* 25(3): 14–17.

Wood, E. and Chesworth, L. (2017) Play and pedagogy. *BERA–TACTYC Early Childhood Research Review*. www.bera.ac.uk/.../bera-tactyc-early-child hood-research-review-2003-2017.

Conclusion and resources/strategies for cultural diversity

In this conclusion each chapter will be summarised and there will be some discussion of the main points, resources and strategies discussed. It will also include references to wider reading that may prove useful and support the reader to know where to access further information about useful ways of working and resources that could be used in practice.

At the heart of this book is the concept of inclusion and the need to view the uniqueness of all children and the families/carers that they grow up with. I make no apologies for this, as I believe it should be at the very heart of all phases of education, from the early years into further and higher education. It is especially important as part of the foundation stone of children's lives that they grow up to see difference as exciting and stimulating rather than viewing it in a negative way.

The first part of the book discussed some of the background knowledge that is important when focusing on any new subject. Although at times this can be a challenge, it is important whenever a new notion is introduced that one carries out research around theory and policy to focus on the historical and theoretical background of education. As this book was evolving it was interesting to acknowledge that even though policies have changed since the 1960s and inclusion has a much greater profile now, the challenges for practitioners remain the same. There is still inadequate training around cultural diversity and the challenges of bilingualism, and parents' expectations of education can still mean that practitioners need to be constantly reflecting on their practice to ensure it meets the needs of all children and families.

The first part of the book also focused on the importance of children discovering and recognising who they are in a positive way. In their early years children pick up information relating to many different aspects of life and through their parents, carers, activities, books and the media they begin to view their world and to experience diversity. If these aspects of their lives are offered positively and in a celebratory way, children will grow up to view difference positively. However, if this is not the case it may impact their views of difference as being more negative through their entire lives.

The second part of the book focused more on the practical aspects of working with families (Chapter 5) and children (Chapter 6). It accentuated the importance of getting alongside all carers/families in a sensitive way, but particularly those families who may be new to the UK. Part II discussed how concepts such as the key person system can ensure that the child, practitioner and family work alongside one another in a non-hierarchical way and also discussed the benefit of bilingual support workers to family and staff. The chapters in Part II also explored some of the many strategies and resources that can support all those involved in early years practice.

Throughout the book I have tried to include concepts and strategies that I view as 'good practice'. This is another principle in the early years that can be confusing. While practitioners are encouraged to offer quality childcare, there are many different views on what good practice looks like. If I was entering a setting expecting to see good practice it would look very different to what another person would expect to observe. This is because it is a subjective term. That means that it relates to each person differently. Because of my interest in inclusion and my experiences of working in both early years practice and higher education, my views on quality practice would be quite different to how an inspector might view the setting. So the resources and strategies that I have suggested in this book will go some way to ensuring that practice in terms of cultural diversity is inclusive.

I hope that the way this book is written will be useful to practitioners and students alike. I have tried to ensure that many of the comments made are validated by further reading, so please use this and the links suggested in this conclusion to support either your studies but particularly your practice with children and families. I suspect that much of this book may introduce concepts and principles that may be new to you. Please take the opportunity to further research these as this in itself will support you in practice and further your knowledge and skills. There may be information in the book that you do not agree with and that may appear to be contrary to your own personal principles; again further research and information may support you to consider these differences in a reflective way that may in time change your views and indeed practice.

Part I

Chapter 1: What is inclusion?

Chapter 1 discussed the importance of inclusion, focusing on how, as a concept, it has changed over the past 50 years and how it has altered over time. It considered differences between the term 'integration' and 'inclusion' and considered how it formerly related in the main to special educational needs (SEN) but now also embraces gender, cultural diversity, sexuality and medical needs.

The chapter continued to suggest that inclusion is not a concept that only one person in a team should be involved with, that person is often the special educational needs co-ordinator (SENCO). It addressed the fact that inclusion is something that should be discussed more strategically as a whole-team approach. The Index for Inclusion was suggested as a resource that can support a team in making changes to the way it works to better include all children and to celebrate their uniqueness. Chapter 1 also suggested that each practitioner has a duty to ensure that practice is inclusive.

Further on in the chapter there was discussion around the role of reflective practice and how this can assist practitioners to consider scenarios, incidents or challenges in practice that need some kind of adjustment. Kolb's reflective cycle was suggested as a good tool for practitioners to use and the chapter also recommended the use of the Development Matters document, which can make the Early Years Foundation Stage a more usable resource.

Finally, the chapter discussed strategies that can be used in practice to enable greater inclusivity. These are personal passports – a strategy first introduced for use with children who are blind but now used with a different range of children to support them particularly through transitions between schools, different agencies and support workers.

The use of Makaton with both children who have special needs or who are bilingual was also discussed. Makaton is an essential tool to use with all young children as it has the potential to open up the world of communication to children who may struggle to make their feelings known. It can also support children with the frustration that goes alongside poor communication.

Finally, the chapter went on to discuss briefly the role of the equalities named co-ordinator (ENCO) and the importance of this role in ensuring that resources used in the setting can be multicultural and how books used can be more appropriate to children from other cultures.

Further reading

Centre for Studies on Inclusive Education (2004) *Index for Inclusion: Developing Participation and Play in Early Years and Childcare.* Bristol: CSIE.

www.csie.org.uk (This website will take you to a lot of useful resources that you can make use of with your team.)

Chapter 2: The political context of cultural diversity

This chapter was dedicated to discussing policy and how it is positioned in terms of cultural diversity. It began by focusing on some of the history of multiculturalism since the 1960s when waves of immigrants began to arrive in the UK. As a result of this, educational policy had to be introduced in order to address some of the challenges of the teaching of thousands of children coming into the UK with little

English and whose parents had no idea about the educational system in the UK. The chapter introduced the Swann Report, which in particular stresses the importance of practitioners gaining knowledge about many of the differences between communities in how they live and carry out their lives.

The United Nations Convention on the Rights of the Child (UNCRC) was then considered, stressing the importance of this legally binding agreement that sets out the civil, political, economic, social and cultural rights of every child. The chapter then went on to question whether the agreement can really address issues of childhood when children live very differently and have access to different resources depending on where in the world they are growing up.

Chapter 2 then discussed the Plowden Report, which was introduced in 1960 and recognised the importance of early years education as we now know it, followed by the the introduction of the Curriculum Guidance for the Foundation Stage in 2000 and then the Early Years Foundation Stage in 2008. The chapter finally introduced the reader to the Prevent Duty introduced in 2015 to try and address issues of radicalisation in the homes of particular communities.

Chapter 3: How does theory relate to cultural diversity?

Through Chapter 3 four differing theories were introduced to the reader. While all of these discuss the importance of the recognition of culture in a child's life, they all take slightly different views on families and children. However, they all support the need for practitioners to carefully reflect on how all children should be treated and encouraged to see difference and diversity as something to celebrate.

The first theorist to be considered was Jerome Bruner. Bruner is recognised for the term 'scaffolding', where adults support children in their learning. Initially an adult might offer a child a lot of support to master a skill, but as the child becomes more confident in their knowledge and ability the adult would ease off their support until the child can achieve independently. This support is particularly important to Bruner as children are developing their communication skills, suggesting that children need adults to encourage them to communicate and help to support them with this important skill. Bruner also introduced the concept of the spiral curriculum, which suggests that children should continue to be introduced to concepts at different points in their lives in order that their knowledge should grow. This enables them to continually add new ideas to existing knowledge.

The ecological systems theory of Urie Bronfenbrenner was then introduced. Bronfenbrenner views children as unique and individual, believing that they grow up in many different contexts and are all 'touched' by many different systems that come and work together. The microsystem is the first of these and sees the child at the centre of their universe. The second is the mesosystem, which includes the child, family, setting, community and religious organisation that the child grows up in. The exosystem is made up of the parent's workplace, extended family and health services that work with the family. Finally the macrosystem includes the laws, customs and values of the country the child grows up in. Bronfenbrenner suggests that these layers do not work in isolation of one another but rather are in relationship with one another.

The chapter went on to discuss the theories of Barbara Rogoff. Rogoff is known as a socioculturalist as she values the cultural aspect of families as a central tenet to their lives. Rogoff has carried out extensive ethnographic research, which is work carried out while living with different cultures to really experience how they live and work. Rogoff suggests that teachers are not the only people to teach children, recommending that children are also taught by their parents, siblings, grandparents as well as by their community elders, priests and religious leaders.

Case study C.1

Peter was 7 years old and had special needs. He had been involved in a road accident when aged 5 and was now in a wheelchair and had some brain damage. The school that he went to had been focusing on different faiths over the term and so had visited many different religious buildings, and speakers such as vicars, Imams and Rabbis had visited the children at school to talk about their work and what was special about the different faiths.

The school was going to a Gurdwara (Sikh temple) to learn about Sikhism and how the temple was used. As the children entered the temple they had to remove their shoes and socks and were taken upstairs to the worship area. After the visit to the worship area the children came downstairs and were provided with a meal of curry and rice.

David was particularly keen to listen to all that the Ragi (Sikh minister) told the children about the faith. For weeks afterwards he asked if the class could return to the Gurdwara to speak to the Ragi again or to invite him back to the school.

This case study reiterates the importance of children visiting different faith traditions and learning about what the different faiths mean.

Reflection

- Have you ever taken children in your setting out into the community to find out what goes on in different parts of it?

- Have you ever taken children in your setting out to different places of worship to find out similarities and differences in faith communities?

- Have you ever asked anyone from a faith group to come in to talk to the children about their faith?

Rogoff also makes the suggestion that different cultures have different 'cultural tools' and artefacts that represent where children grow up. In the West these might be seen as pens, pencils, nursery rhymes, fairy stories, folklore, music and art. However, for children in other parts of the world these may be different – she suggests that children in Africa may be more used to using twigs and mud, whereas children in the UK would use paint and brushes. Rogoff contends that all countries have different art and music that are representative of that culture.

The final theorist discussed was Liz Brooker. She has carried out a lot of research in relation to culture and much of this has focused on play and the view that families from across the world may not value the use of play in learning as we do in the West. Brooker also discusses the importance of the environment in terms of giving children cues to what they may do in different areas and with different tools. Brooker also introduces to practice a concept known as the 'triangle of care'. This is a non-hierarchical structure that ensures the sharing of information between the parents, child and practitioner.

Chapter 4: Who are we? The impact of cultural diversity on a child's identity

The final chapter of Part I discussed the importance of identity. It suggested that identity is not stable but evolves during the whole of our lives. First, the chapter encouraged the reader to consider what a child is. This is a question that will be answered differently, I suspect, by people of different ages and may seem an obvious one. However, there are and have been many different views on this question. Also, this view will differ depending on what culture one comes from, as the role of a child may be very different depending on where in the world they come from. The chapter continued to explain how children start to build ideas about their own identity and what is important to them in their lives.

The chapter then went on to discuss some of the dilemmas that families travelling across countries have to face and considered some of the experiences that refugees and asylum seekers go through when having to leave their countries of origin. It also tried to demystify stereotypes and views about concepts including the meaning of words such as 'culture', 'religion' and 'spirituality'.

Finally, the chapter discussed the effects of the media, parents and racism and how these can affect how children growing up form their own identity.

Further reading

bernardvanleer.org/ (An essential resource for further information about culture and identity, as they produce a lot of free resources related to Chapter 4.)

Part II

Chapter 5: Working with families

This chapter began with a look at some of the historical changes in the role of the family and how the structure of the family has changed, particularly over the past 50–60 years. It sought to compare the role of the family in the UK to that of people living in other cultures, and introduced a concept called 'cultural intelligence' (CQ) that can be used to support practitioners to better understand how people from other cultures live and work.

It then continued to demystify concepts, particularly those used across the media to 'label' those who come to the UK from other cultures. These labels may seem to some to be quite negative and pejorative but they seek to classify people at various stages of their journey in the UK. It is therefore important that early years practitioners have some understanding of what they mean.

The next part of the chapter focused on what the EYFS has to say about the work that is carried out in settings with parents while also addressing some of the safeguarding issues that might emerge when parents living in new communities and countries do not fully understand safeguarding laws in the UK. Finally, the chapter discussed the importance of the key person in early years practice and how they can get alongside and support families to feel welcome in their new communities.

Chapter 6: Working with young children

Chapter 6 opened with some discussion of the importance of an enabling environment. This has been at the heart of the EYFS since its development and reminds the practitioner that children pick up a lot of cues from the setting environment, the way it is set up and the resources available for children to learn and explore, particularly if they are bilingual or struggling to communicate in a different way. The role of the outdoors was discussed and the value of open resources in all areas of the setting was extolled.

The chapter continued to discuss the view that cultural diversity can be used as a resource for learning. This may make some people quite dubious about discussing difference and diversity openly with children. However, it is important for children to learn, early on in their lives that we are all different. This can be done through painting and drawing activities where children are asked to paint or draw themselves and say how they are different to others in the group. It can also be done through stories. Many of the books suggested earlier in the chapter relate to how people are and how they might be feeling and can be an introduction to a discussion about ourselves and how we are all different from one another.

The importance of communication was discussed and a strategy called 'RAMPS' introduced as a reflective way of thinking about communication in settings. It is a fairly quick and easy activity that could be discussed in a team meeting to ensure that your setting takes care to provide children with all that they need to effectively communicate.

Alongside this discussion was the recognition that some children who may be bilingual or who struggle to communicate orally may need augmentative communication strategies such as Makaton to help them to communicate with one another. Two important concepts that need to be addressed with children were also introduced – 'agency' and 'participation'. At times it can be difficult to see these terms as different. Agency relates to the opportunities that practitioners give to children through choices and participation is about the ability adults give children to have a say in things that involve them.

Finally, the chapter discussed the challenges of bilingualism to children and staff and what can be done to support children who are learning two languages alongside each other. It considered the silent period when children may choose to stop communicating with others and offered support through resources such as the Mosaic approach. Finally, the chapter extolled the use of bilingual workers in settings with high numbers of children from other cultures and the way they can support children, their families and practitioners.

Chapter 6 discussed the importance of inclusion in a child's life, emphasising that if at the beginning of life children learn about difference in a positive way, this will then set an important foundation stone for the rest of their lives. The Early Years Foundation Stage document is a fundamental document that sets out the need for children to celebrate their uniqueness and should, I believe, be at the heart of all services offered to families and children across the country, whether or not they are in multicultural communities. The chapter went on to recognise the need for practitioners to work closely with families and introduced a number of sociocultural theories that acknowledge that all families live differently from one another and that no one group of families are superior to another. The chapter also introduced the importance of a child's culture to how children start to view and establish their identity.

Various strategies have also been presented that can support practice in order to make it more inclusive. The chapter summarised the benefits of the Index for Inclusion as a strategic tool to evaluate practice and to set up new ways of working. The benefits of using Makaton in settings were discussed as this can benefit children learning English for the first time as well as those with speech and language difficulties. The benefits of using cultural intelligence as a lens to view the lives of people were also explored, showing how this tool may help you as a practitioner to understand a little more about how and why groups of people live differently.

It is my hope that practitioners may investigate and use some of these strategies in practice, to ensure that settings become more inclusive to the needs of all families and children.

Further reading

www.communityplaythings.co.uk/learning-library/articles/open-ended-play?topic=B48B04502C6945709E480E3FB5C6A5CC (An interesting booklet that gives tips to practitioners about open-ended play can be found here.)

www.ncb.org.uk/sites/default/files/field/.../Ready%20to%20listen%20 2016.pdf (Provides a useful resource from the National Children's Bureau about the importance of being ready to listen to children.)

Index

3003204